THE KEY ISSUES LECTURE SERIES
is made possible through a grant from
International Telephone and Telegraph Corporation

SOCIAL
RESPONSIBILITY
AND ACCOUNTABILITY

Edited by
Jules Backman

With a Foreword by
Harold S. Geneen

New York: New York University Press   1975

Library of Congress Catalog Card Number: 75-10902

ISBN: 0-8147-1000-X (cloth)
ISBN: 0-8147-1002-6 (paper)

Manufactured in the United States of America

Library of Congress Cataloging in Publication Data
Main entry under title:

Social responsibility and accountability

   (Key issues lecture series)
   A lecture series of the College of Business and Public
Administration, New York University.
   Includes bibliographical references.
   1. Industry—Social aspects—Addresses, essays,
lectures.   2. Industry—Social aspects—United States—
Addresses, essays, lectures.   I. Backman, Jules,
1910-   II. New York University. College of Business
and Public Administration.
HD60.S6   301.5'1   75-10902

Preface

Abraham L. Gitlow

Dean

College of Business and Public Administration
New York University

This volume is the fourth in the Key Issues Lecture Series at the College of Business and Public Administration, New York University. The series, which was made possible by a grant from the International Telephone and Telegraph Corporation, has received wide and favorable review, amply confirming our original expectations that it would make a significant contribution to public understanding of a number of major contemporary issues.

The lectures published herein represent the eight-part series discussing various aspects of "social responsibility". In this volume Professor Jules Backman, its editor and the organizer of the Key Issues Lecture Series, has brought together the thinking of eight outstanding minds. That such is the case has been richly demonstrated by the extraordinary coverage given the lectures as well as by the significant discussion engendered by them. We are profoundly grateful to the contributors, as well as to Jules Backman, for these most successful lectures.

I would be delinquent if I failed also to express appreciation to Mrs. Catherine Ferfoglia, who is Professor Backman's secretary and who helped prepare the volume for publication; to my administrative assistants, Mrs. Patricia Matthias and Mrs. Virginia Moress.

Contents

Foreword

Harold S. Geneen

Chairman and Chief Executive
International Telephone and Telegraph Corporation

The definition of corporate social responsibility has become increasingly clouded as movements such as consumerism and environmentalism have collided with the tides of economic change, and the creation of jobs and economic stability has reemerged as the primary role of private enterprise.

In this climate, questions arise as to how business can promote the sometimes conflicting interests of society and build a better life for individuals.

Every enterprise thus has the difficult responsibility to act, as far as possible, so it does not damage one element of society while serving another. Yet, decisions related to the assignment of priorities and the balancing of objectives in the social sphere increasingly are being dictated by government, economics, and other outside factors, with a resultant diminishing role for the corporation in determining its own contribution.

The obligations attendant to corporate social responsibility, and their performance, therefore demand informed discussion in a public forum.

That need is served effectively by the lectures in this volume, originally presented at New York University as the Key Issues Lecture Series.

During these lectures, the issues were probed from the viewpoints of business, the economist, the social scientist, the educator, the investor, and the professions.

This is the broad range of perspective needed to deal with these diverse aspects of corporate social responsibilities, particularly at a time when societies are being assaulted by economic difficulty, and business enterprise is being held responsible for current problems while the true causes are often overlooked.

The important and timely question concerns the future role of the corporation in society, and this forum of opinion is directed toward that purpose.

ITT is pleased to have sponsored these lectures, and we express our appreciation to Dr. Jules Backman for organizing the programs and for compiling and editing this volume.

We are also grateful to the audiences—especially the students of New York University—whose observations and questions have contributed importantly to the dialogue initiated by these lectures.

THE KEY ISSUES LECTURE SERIES
is made possible through a grant from
International Telephone and Telegraph Corporation

ONE

Social Responsibility:
The Problem and Its Setting *

Jules Backman

Research Professor of Economics
New York University

During the past decade, there has been considerable public pressure
on American business to give increasing attention to its social responsibilities. Throughout our history, the major thrusts of business have
been upon growth in sales and in profits. In the pursuit of these
objectives, significant social costs simultaneously incurred were ignored or overlooked. For example, plants polluted the streams with
their waste and the air with their use and production of energy. And
communities in their search for sources of employment and higher tax
rolls competed vigorously for these plants without counting the total
social costs, including pollution. What is now taking place is a shift in
priorities, with more emphasis given to social responsibility.

As often happens, we have moved to the other extreme, particularly
in the area of pollution control. This is well illustrated by the many
ways in which our concern over pollution has inhibited our ability to

* My special thanks to Marvin Levine, who provided valuable assistance in the
collection of materials for this chapter.

achieve a much-needed expansion in domestic supplies of energy. The basic policy question is: Can we undo in a few years, the practices which were acceptable for many decades? Or should we set the necessary and desirable goals and "make haste more slowly" in reaching them?

To what extent will the initiative to solve the problems—grouped under the heading of social responsibility—come from business? To what extent from government? The broad goals must be established by government but their effective implementation requires the full cooperation of business. This cooperation will be more easily mobilized by use of the carrot rather than the stick. As Professor Juanita Kreps suggests: "In order to gain voluntary compliance, means must be devised to persuade the corporation to accept the responsibility as a legitimate business activity."

Probably the most important reason for using incentives to solve the problems involved is the complexity of business and the consequent need for a diversity of solutions. As Lee Loevinger has concluded:

> those who must translate policies into actions know that the simple, easy solutions are seldom practical or effective. . . .
> Certainly no specific detailed program will serve all business. But it is equally clear that every business will eventually be required to produce its own plan for ascertaining the social needs with which it must deal.[1]

Some Definitions

Social responsibility, social accounting, social indicators, and social audit—these terms cover different facets of what may be called *social performance*. At the present time, these definitions are general rather than precise. It is only after we have had considerable experience in attempts to quantify each concept that the full range of problems of measurement will be understood. But if we don't take the first crude steps, we will make no progress.

Social responsibility usually refers to the *objectives or motives* that should be given weight by business in addition to those dealing with economic performance (e.g., profits). Employment of minority groups, reduction in pollution, greater participation in programs to improve the community, improved medical care, improved industrial health and safety—these and other programs designed to improve the *quality* of life are covered by the broad umbrella of social responsibility. (See Chapters 2 and 3.)

Social accounting is concerned with developing a *broad measurement* of what is happening to the quality of life. This measurement would be a companion index to gross national product (GNP), which provides our broadest measure of *the quantity of life* even though, as Professor Morgenstern shows (Chapter 4), it suffers from many deficiencies. Although some attempts have been made to expand the coverage of GNP into a Measure of Economic Welfare (MEW),[2] we appear to be a long distance away from being able to summarize all aspects of quality of life in a single figure as we do for economic activity.

Social indicators describe a group of measures that show the quality of life—for example, extent of poverty, number of industrial accidents, number of welfare recipients, social mobility, degree of pollution, extent of education, and extent of health services. In combination, they give a broad picture of what is happening to many phases of the quality of life. (See Chapter 5.)

Finally, the *corporate social audit* refers to attempts to measure the social performance of a company by listing and measuring the various actions it takes or fails to take in the area of social responsibility. (See Chapter 6.)

CORPORATE SOCIAL RESPONSIBILITY

Real gross national product and real disposable income have increased significantly over the years. This economic growth has been accompanied by increasing levels of employment, of wages, of fringe benefits, and of expanding career opportunities for many. Millions of shareholders of corporations and holders of life insurance policies and pensions have shared in this growth. Resources available to governments have been increased significantly by the income and wealth that has been generated by our prodigious economic system.

The dynamic nature of the private enterprise economy has encouraged business to expand and to innovate. The drive for profits encourages business to develop new and improved products and to lower costs. As a result, we have obtained the means as well as the leisure to enjoy the better life.[3] The competitive marketplace in a capitalistic economy serves as an effective instrument to develop an efficient allocation of resources in response to the needs and wants of the society.

Dr. James Hester points out: "Today, the corporation is undergoing the most intensive public scrutiny in its history. It has been alleged that they are little concerned about the interests of the consumer, are indifferent to the deteriorating social order, and are dangerous polluters of the environment." Nevertheless, many companies have recognized the importance of social responsibility.[4]

However, increasingly there has developed a cleavage between those who opt for the corporation to emphasize its role to be that of making profits and those who would give increasing emphasis in the affairs of the modern-day business to noneconomic pursuits. Milton Friedman has emphasized the primacy of the business firm's drive for profits,[5] while the late Eli Goldston, a leading business spokesman for broader social responsibility, has taken the latter approach.[6]

John Diebold has suggested an intermediate position that would use the profit motive to achieve agreed upon social goals:

> The right way to bring about the required switch in production to social priorities is for the government to establish incentives and constraints in such a way that profit is made doing what society most needs to be done in a manner that society finds acceptable.[7]

Actually, the role of business has never been at the extremes of ignoring completely its social responsibility or of being guided completely by that goal. As Professor Juanita Kreps points out:

> What is different today is not that people are suddenly demanding actions of business, whereas in the past business was free to respond only to market forces. Business has always been obligated to observe the rules laid down by the public's elected representatives. Rather, the difference lies in the degree to which

business is now asked to interpret the public's preferences and to formulate courses of action to implement these preferences, even before governmental action has stipulated what should be done.

There has been and likely will continue to be a philosophical shift from unbridled self-interest to enlightened social interest. The growing concern over social responsibility by business in essence illustrates the adaptive capacity of the capitalistic system. Emphasis upon social responsibility is the newest scene in a long drama in which a free economic system adjusts to the demands made upon it.

Pollution Control: A Key Area

A decrease in pollution unquestionably will increase the quality of life, and this is a most desirable goal to achieve. We must recognize, however, that there will be a cost, and we must be ready to pay the cost. The Council of Economic Advisers has stated:

> The fundamental premise of economic policy is that the Nation's total resources must be allocated as efficiently as possible. This concept includes careful allocation of our scarce environmental resources, but it does not follow that environmental policy should be insulated from other problems and policies.[8]

There are several elements to be noted:

(1) The available supply of funds for new investment is limited. Therefore, the funds that are used to eliminate pollution cannot also be used to expand capacity. Table 1 shows the relationship between expenditures for pollution control and for total plant and equipment.

(2) In a number of industries including cement, chemicals, paper, and iron and steel, older plants have been shut down because of the high cost of meeting pollution standards. For example, the cement industry has estimated it would cost around $200 million to reduce pollution at profitable plants. In the chemical industry, some companies have been spending in excess of 10 percent of their capital

Table 1

Relationship Between Pollution Control
and Plant and Equipment Spending,
1971–1974

	Expenditures on Pollution Control	Plant and Equipment Spending	Percent re-lationship
	[billions]		
1971	$3.2	$81.2	3.9%
1972	4.9	88.4	5.5
1973	5.7	99.7	5.7
1974	7.4	112.7	6.6

Sources: McGraw-Hill Economics Department and U.S. Department of Commerce, Bureau of Economic Analysis.

budgets for the required equipment.[9] Investment in antipollution control equipment was estimated at over one and one half billion dollars a year for electric utilities in 1974 in contrast to slightly more than one half billion dollars two years earlier.[10]. This has been quite a burden during a period when huge financial requirements to meet greater demand have been difficult to finance in the inflation ridden capital markets. Electric power consumers also were adversely affected when companies were prevented from using lower cost fuels, which were less pollutant free, when oil prices got out of hand in 1973–74.

Professor Kreps points out that business cannot resolve this conflict between the need for more energy and possible environmental pollution. She questions whether

the corporation is particularly well equipped to interpret the public's wishes and to direct the allocation of resources into socially desirable projects. Beyond responding to consumer preference expressed in the market place and public sentiment expressed in governmental directive, which sets of signals is business to answer? If environmentalists argue for cleaner air and consumers for more fuel, is there any resolution except by democratic rule?

(3) Clearly, one of the costs of a better quality of life will be a lower rate of increase in our levels of living. The diversion of investment funds and R & D to pollution control is significant in this connection as is the reduction in capacity noted above. In 1972, total expenditures for pollution control and abatement were $18,738 million of which $1,585 million was for R & D.[11]

(4) The pollution problem has developed over a period of many decades. The attempts to eradicate it in a relatively short period of time creates excessive stresses and strains on the economy and may involve an unwise use of resources. Is zero pollution worth the cost that must be met to attain it? Economists always are concerned with alternative uses of resources. As John R. Meyer has noted:

the resources that may be squandered on this pursuit of an idealized perfection are likely to be resources that *may* not be available for other very worthy purposes, such as reduction of poverty or improvement of our educational system.[12]

A longer time span must be permitted to achieve the desired goals of abating pollution. The important point is that we must move rapidly in the right direction rather than hope to resolve this problem instantaneously. In this area as with many economic problems there is no "instant cure."

MEASUREMENT OF SOCIAL RESPONSIBILITY

Three of the contributions to this volume deal with the problems of measurement. Professor Oskar Morgenstern is concerned with the economic approach, namely, the usefulness of GNP as a measurement (Chapter 4). Robert Parke and Eleanor B. Sheldon spell out the emerging area of social indicators (Chapter 5), and David Linowes offers some useful suggestions as to how to measure the contributions to social responsibility by the corporation (Chapter 6).

GNP as a Measure of Social Welfare

The most comprehensive measure of economic activity is GNP. There is no identity between the level of economic activity and social welfare, although there is a relationship between the two, as the contrast between the American economy and those in the underdeveloped areas of the world clearly demonstrates. Professor Morgenstern spells out many limitations to GNP even as a measure of economic performance. (See Chapter 4.) In addition to the problems of measurement, however, there are also serious problems of coverage if GNP is to be used to measure social welfare.

Among the coverage limitations of GNP are the failure to place any value on leisure, the exclusion of goods and services that do not involve money transactions, and the failure to allow for the disamenities that have developed. Thus, a reduction in the length of the workday and the workweek over the years as well as an increase in vacation time is not reflected in total gross national product. Unpaid services of housewives are excluded. The satisfaction or lack of it that people obtain from their work is not measured. The growing industrialization and urbanization have brought such negative aspects as pollution and ecological costs, which are not evaluated in gross national product even though they are an important element in social welfare.

Nordhaus and Tobin have endeavored to take into consideration the most significant differences between GNP and economic welfare in their measure of economic welfare (MEW):

Conceptually [it] is a comprehensive measure of the annual real consumption of households. Consumption is intended to include all goods and services, marketed or not, valued at market prices or at their equivalent in opportunity costs to consumers. Collective public consumption is to be included, whether provided by government or otherwise; and allowance is to be made for negative externalities, such as those due to environmental damage and to the disamenities and congestion of urbanization and industrialization. Real consumption is estimated by valuing the flows of goods and services at constant prices.[13]

Although such an index would provide a closer approximation to a measure of welfare, it still falls far short of the goal being sought. In fact, there is serious question whether we can measure welfare for this country in a single figure. As Professor Morgenstern concludes:

> "Social welfare" is still so difficult and controversial a notion that, without overcoming the inherent great conceptual difficulties we cannot indicate any measure at present which is scientifically unchallengeable and does not involve political, moral, or whatever other prejudices.

Social Indicators

Economic reporting has been far more advanced in all countries with much less attention given to measuring changes in the quality of life. Social progress obviously does not result when a rise in crime brings about the manufacture of an increased number of burglar alarms and with it a rise in GNP. In recent years, there has developed growing interest in taking the social pulse of countries throughout the world both to monitor social progress and to help governments formulate social policy. Social reporting has been more developed in Great Britain and Japan than in the United States.

Social indicators can furnish much useful information.[14] The finer the detailed breakdowns, the more meaningful the indicators. Social reporting can show interrelationships that may turn out to be a very important area of interest. This may be illustrated by the relationship that exists between the educational level of young people and their opportunity to obtain and hold jobs.

The developing interest in social indicators is reflected in the comprehensive report issued by the Office of Management and Budget's Statistical Policy Division in 1973. This report "contains a collection of statistics selected and organized to describe social conditions and trends in the United States." It examined eight major areas: health, public safety, education, employment, income, housing, leisure and recreation, and population. For each of these categories, social concerns are discussed. Thus, in the health sphere the areas "are long life, life free from disability, and access to medical care."

The OMB study points out that:

an indicator would reveal not only the status of the population in relation to a perceived social objective, but it would also furnish some idea of what forces were influencing that status. At the present time, not enough is known about the cause and effect of social conditions to develop such ideal indicators. Rather, the indicators presented in this publication represent simply a first step toward the development of a more extensive social indicator system.[15]

Drs. Parke and Sheldon describe the relationship between social indicators and corporate responsibility and conclude:

The role of social indicators in the development of the measurement of corporate performance is not in their usefulness for priority setting or program evaluation; it rests rather in the promise to provide answers to a few simple questions: What does our society look like? How is it changing, and why? We trust that this is a significant role.

CORPORATE SOCIAL AUDIT

The development of the concept of the social responsibility of business makes it imperative that criteria be developed to measure the performance by business in areas of broad social concern. The corporate social audit is the proposed method of measurement.[16]

The purpose of a corporate social audit is to "help break down all or a large part of the broad term, social responsibility of business, into identifiable components, and to develop scales that can measure these components." [17]

In Chapter 6, David F. Linowes has proposed setting up a Socio-Economic Operating Statement (SEOS) which would include:

1. A tabulation of those expenditures made voluntarily by a

business aimed at improving the welfare of employees and public; safety of the product; and conditions of the environment.

2. Costs of socially beneficial items which have been brought to the attention of management, and which a reasonably prudent socially aware management would be expected to undertake, but this management chooses to ignore.

Mr. Linowes omits from his SEOS any expenditures which are "required by law or union contract." He is concerned only with voluntary actions. The omission of mandatory expenditures would mean that the SEOS does not show fully what a company is doing in this area. For example, an electric utility may be required to spend tens of millions of dollars to reduce or to eliminate air pollution. Such an expenditure would represent an overwhelming contribution to the area of social responsibility by a company, yet it would not be included in the SEOS. At the minimum, Linowes' SEOS should include a comprehensive note describing these mandatory expenditures, so that a more complete picture of a company's actions is obtained.

It must be recognized at the outset that any attempt to establish a "balance sheet" of debits and credits in the area of social responsibility will be very crude. There will be problems of measurement, of identification of pertinent areas of coverage, and related questions. But unless a start is made toward the corporate social audit, the more refined tools will not ultimately be developed. This problem is not unique to this area. The early measures of gross national product also were very crude. But as scholars analyzed the problems of measurement and resolved conflicting theories concerning the treatment of important components, the GNP has become more comprehensive and a more useful measure of trends in our economy. The more we are aware of the inadequacies of our early measurements, the more quickly the more refined techniques for corporate social audits will be developed.

Though it is still very difficult to measure the cost of social programs in precise terms, some efforts have been made to do so. Such an audit would be most helpful to the public and other interested groups who are concerned with what is being done by a business and how much is being spent to carry out various social programs. In the absence of such reports, it has been relatively easy for the critics of business to pollute the minds of the public by repeating constantly the theme that the corporations are not concerned about communities and their problems, but are only interested in profits. Thus, no useful purpose is to be served by the business community if it keeps quiet and does not report the particulars of its role in social programs.

The social audit must be thought of in relation to the broader subject of the social responsibility of business. The audit is the measure of the responsibility.

SOME SPECIAL SECTORS: MEDICINE, INVESTMENTS, AND MULTINATIONAL COMPANIES

Much of the literature concerned with social responsibility either is general in nature or deals with specific practices which it is proposed to change (e.g., pollution, job discrimination, consumer victimization). However, social responsibility has different effects and requires varying approaches in different segments of the economy. The final three chapters illustrate these differences in medicine (Chapter 7), portfolio decisions (Chapter 8), and multinational companies (Chapter 9).

Social Responsibility and Social
Accountability in Medicine

National health expenditures have increased tremendously in recent decades. A continuation of this trend seems likely for the balance of the 1970s. Both on a per capita basis and as a percent of gross national product, the rise has been dramatic. (See Table 2.)

This spectacular rise has reflected a combination of the higher prices for medical services, the growth of population, easier access to medical care, the increase in the number of elderly persons who need greater medical care, and the improvements in the quality of the services available, such as renal dialysis, organ transplants, etc.

Medical services have rather unique characteristics. Thus, the physician occupies a special role—he furnishes services directly to the

Table 2

Health Expenditures, Per Capita and as Percent of Gross National
Product, Selected Years 1929–1974

Fiscal Year	Health Expend. [millions]	Per Capita	Percent of GNP
1929	$3,589	$29.16	3.6%
1940	3,863	28.83	4.1
1950	12,028	78.35	4.6
1960	25,856	141.63	5.2
1970	69,202	333.57	7.2
1974	104,239	485.36	7.7

Source: Nancy L. Worthington, "National Health Expenditures, 1929–74," *Social Security Bulletin* (February 1975), p. 5.

consumer and determines the services that he requires from others such as hospitals and suppliers of medicines. Traditionally, it has been the doctor who decides the medications, the number of days to be spent in the hospital, and the special services that are required.[18] The consumer usually has little or no knowledge about medical services. There is a paucity of objective information available to him about the quality of available medical care. Prices of medical services may not be known to the buyer until the bill is received.

It has been suggested that the high cost of medical care could be reduced through the use of paramedical personnel to do some of the work traditionally handled by physicians. The results would be a more economical use of the physician's time that would increase his productivity, lower costs, and increase the supply of medical services. Greater utilization of group practice also has been advocated as a means of sharing costs and revenues. Under some existing arrangements, medical services are furnished to consumers at prepaid fixed fees and thus there is an incentive to provide services at the lowest possible cost, as the group's net income varies inversely with the cost of furnishing in services.[19]

It is against this background that increasing attention is being given to social responsibility and accountability in medicine. As Dr. Harry

Schwartz points out, historically the law of malpractice provided the major protection for patients [Chapter 7]. In recent years, malpractice suits have been used successfully and have resulted in such large payments that many insurance companies became unwilling to write such insurance and the leading insurer requested astronomical increases in insurance premium costs; for some doctors the proposed premium was increased to more than $50,000 a year. In addition, it was reported that many doctors began to practice "defensive medicine", that is to require many more tests than normally would be needed, in order to protect themselves against malpractice claims.

These developments contributed to a significant rise in medical costs and also threatened to act as a barrier to entry into some specialties by many young doctors. As a result, some states enacted legislation to make available malpractice insurance at more reasonable premiums and to develop less costly approaches than jury trials to determine the proper level of damages.

For example, in April 1975 Indiana passed a law which provided for a ceiling of $500,000 on damages in any single case, created a medical review panel to issue a formal opinion as a condition for filing a malpractice suit, limited a doctor's liability to a maximum of $100,000 in any single malpractice case and created a state compensation fund to pay damage awards in excess of $100,000 to be financed by a surcharge of not more than 10% in malpractice insurance premiums. Maryland enacted a law which set a five-year statute of limitations for malpractice claims.[20]

The large-scale involvement in medical care by government through Medicare and Medicaid and the sharply rising level of such costs have led to the demand for strict accountability for the funds spent. As a result, Congress provided in October 1972 for the establishment of Professional Standards Review Organizations (PSRO). The main role of the PSROs, which will be established throughout the country, is "to impose accountability upon physicians, accountability primarily to the government with respect to services for which it pays."

Dr. Schwartz spells out in considerable detail the problems which will beset this approach and raises important questions concerning its effect upon the delivery of good medical care.

When governments spend large sums of money, it is necessary and unavoidable that every effort must be made to ensure that such funds are spent wisely and efficiently. The implementation of this goal is very difficult for medical care because it is delivered on a person to person basis and the quality of the diagnosis and care prescribed is vitally important. Here is the key problem with PSRO. All types of medical care cannot be predetermined within rigid parameters. Progress in medicine requires experimentation with new techniques that are not listed in a PSRO manual and hence may not be reimbursable. The flexibility with which the PSRO approach is handled will determine its success in resolving this problem.

Portfolio Decisions and Social Responsibility

The growing concern over social responsibility has been accompanied by demands that this factor be given weight in portfolio decision making particularly for nonprofit organizations such as universities, hospitals, and religious institutions. Investment advisers have been requested to consider the extent to which companies in which they plan to invest are socially responsible. This adds a new dimension to the already difficult task of selecting investments.

Some institutions have announced that their investment policy will consider the social responsibility of companies in which they hold securities. In June 1971, the Board of Trustees of the Ford Foundation adopted an investment policy based upon the following general principle:

> Investment decisions shall be made so as to sustain and strengthen the capacity of the Foundation to effectuate its purpose and to serve the general welfare of the people.[21]

Similarly, the trustees of Harvard University adopted the following policy statement in May 1972:

> The Trustees believe the University, as an investor, must focus not only on a maximum economic return, but also on issues of social responsibility, as produced by the company in which the University holds securities. Harvard's definition of "social responsibility" encompasses such areas as a company's position on

or involvement in labor relations, racial discrimination, minority employment practices, consumer protection, pollution control, military contracts and international diplomacy.[22]

Other institutions of higher learning have been requested by various groups to emphasize social responsibility. Thus, at Princeton and Cornell investments in companies operating in South Africa have been challenged, at Dartmouth and Union College controversy has arisen over Eastman-Kodak's minority hiring policy, and at the University of Pennsylvania the issue developed over demands made upon General Motors.[23]

Mutual funds also have been affected by this development. At a meeting of the Fidelity Fund, it was requested that the company give careful consideration to the civil rights and pollution records of the firms that were being considered for investment. This proposal received about one out of every eight votes cast.[24]

That investors generally have not been willing to give very much weight to corporate actions in the area of social responsibility is indicated by the liquidation of the Spectrum Fund, Inc., in 1974. This fund had been formed several years earlier to invest in the securities of "socially responsible corporations." It found relatively few investors who were ready to put their money into the fund. Thomas N. Daley, Jr., one of the founders, reported:

We found little real support from those investors we had every reason to believe shared our concerns about corporate responsibility, and whom we fully expected would make at least some commitment, even a token amount, in our fund. It was in failing to persuade church organizations, college endowments, certain pension funds, foundations, and their respective members, to invest in our concept that ultimately resulted in our having to give it up; if we couldn't attract them into the fund, whom could we attract? . . . We ended it confirmed skeptics, seriously questioning whether anyone really cares about anything to do with investments other than how much they will make, which is, of course, where the true skeptics have been all along.[25]

Portfolio decisions that give heavy weight to social responsibility can be fairly costly to an institution under some conditions. In this connection, an ad hoc committee (headed by Professor Burton A. Malkiel) on Princeton's investments in companies operating in South Africa emphasized in 1969 that if

> Princeton were to sell its shares in 38 companies with affiliates and subsidiaries in South Africa, and if the return provided by these companies continued to bear the same relationship to the rest of the securities available for investment, the divestment would impose on Princeon a one-time transaction cost of approximately $5 million attributable to brokerage charges and "blockage"-related costs.[26]

The implementation of an investment policy that gives great weight to a corporation's social responsibility is very difficult. How shall a company's social performance be measured? Who shall determine what is socially responsible behavior? Often there is considerable disagreement concerning some proposed policies. For example, should a company's board include a "public interest representative" (as advocated for General Motors) or representatives of minority groups? Are investments in South Africa a matter to be dealt with through foreign policy or investment policy? Often it will take a number of years to correct an abuse or it will require the investment of huge sums. Pollution control is a good illustration. Who will determine if a company is moving rapidly enough to eliminate pollution?

Shall a company be condemned for any deviation from some groups' concept of socially desirable behavior or will we strike a balance between good deeds and bad? Every company probably engages in some activity which will be evaluated critically by some persons—and the larger the company the greater the probability that the company will find itself in this situation. The policy statement for one religious educational institution attempts to deal with this problem as follows:

> Only if the corporation is directly and *substantially* involved in activities clearly considered by the college's administration and its board to be contrary to *fundamental and widely shared ethical principles*

should the investment counsel be instructed to avoid purchase of its securities.

If an investor is unhappy about a corporation's activities or lack of them in the area of social responsibility what should he do? Vote his proxy against management? Submit a resolution condemning the action of the annual meeting? Or should he sell his stock? The investor does have options. In most instances, however, an individual or an institution holds such a relatively unimportant proportion of the stock that no leverage can be exerted. Obviously, only if large numbers of investors shun a company's stock can there be any effect on a company's policy.

Finally, the question should be raised whether excessive attention is being given to social responsibility in the selection of securities. For a corporation to be successful over time, it must recognize changing social and economic forces. The companies that make the adjustments tend to become the industry leaders and tend to provide profitable investment opportunities. Doesn't the emphasis really belong upon the capibility and farsightedness of management rather than upon policies that become socially unacceptable because of a change in public attitudes toward some practices that were acceptable in the past?

Social Responsibility and the Multinational Company

The far-flung nature of their operations inevitably involve the multinational corporation (MNC) in activities extending beyond the drive for profits. Thus, it has been pointed out that the influence of the MNC "can be a strong force for modernization within a country. It can contribute directly to better education, improved health conditions, and housing." [27] The multinational corporation must learn much about the environment in foreign nations where it operates so that its policies can be developed accordingly. [28]

Increasingly, the multinational corporation has come under attack in foreign lands for its emphasis on immediate profits. It is charged that the MNC has very remote ties to the host country and is not concerned with its specific problems. To overcome this image, some MNCs have moved to place more importance on the well-being of the countries in which they operate than on quick profits, to take an interest in community problems, and to give nationals opportunities for positions with meaningful responsibility and prestige. This approach must be submitted to periodic review to be certain that new forces are not undermining the goals.

The multinational company faces a broader variety of social responsibility problems than does a domestic company. In addition to the domestic social responsibilities involving the environment, consumerism, equal opportunity, working conditions, etc., it must be concerned with a number of areas that are peculiar to a company operating in another country. These include their handling of foreign exchange transactions, competitive activities vis-à-vis local companies, "tax morality," extent of local ownership, cultural erosion, and others.

Dean Ingo Walter notes that the MNC "operates in multiple social, political settings, each with a different historical pattern of development, set of current conditions, and collectively-determined national goal structure." Moreover, "acceptable business behavior in any one country may also run counter to public policy or group interest elsewhere." As a result, the MNC finds that "a uniform set of global policies targeted on social issues seems out of the question."

Dean Walter points out that the MNC has three alternative policies it can follow in meeting its social responsibilities in each country:

> 1. Compliance-oriented behavior, which involves "strict adherence to legal and administrative constraints and to the rules of the marketplace without substantial voluntarism."
> 2. Selective voluntarism, which involves "the development of a baseline corporate policy targeted on specific social responsibility issues that can be modified efficiently to meet often poorly defined local conditions."
> 3. Avoidance-oriented behavior, which arises "in part from the fundamental characteristics of multinationalism" and "cannot be alleviated either by strict compliance with externally-imposed constraints or through voluntary alignment of corporate policies with prevailing social objectives."

The manner in which the MNC moves to meet its social responsibilities will depend upon which of these policies it follows. Of course, it may adopt varying approaches in different countries depending in part upon the local management and the pressures generated in each country. In this connection, there may be conflicts in the social objectives of one nation with others in such matters as full employment, environmental considerations, job discrimination, and balance of payments. In addition, as Raymond Vernon has noted, "there may be conflicts between what is good for mankind as a whole and what is good for each country taken one at a time." [29]

Nevertheless, an effort must be made to bring some uniformity in social responsibility goals among countries. For example, it may be relatively less costly to produce in countries that remain unconcerned about environmental problems than in countries where efforts are made to clean up the environment. To overcome this problem it may be necessary to adopt international standards,[30] a very difficult objective to achieve.

COST-BENEFIT ANALYSIS

The goals sought under the broad umbrella of social responsibility represent desirable objectives in many instances. However, their achievement often will involve significant costs. To the extent that resources are required to reduce pollution, to improve product safety, to improve working conditions, and to make progress in other areas of social irresponsibility, there will be a cost—sometimes a very heavy cost. Included in these costs are large expenditures for capital investment, the diversion of manpower and the high cost of paper work for implementation, and the cost to government of regulation.[31] The price we must pay for a better quality of life in part will be a slower rate of increase in our levels of living in quantitative terms.

Too often the goals to be achieved are emphasized while the costs are muted or ignored. But a rational approach requires a consideration of both the costs and benefits of a program. For example, are we willing to pay a much higher price for electric power for forgoing the use of high-sulfur coal with its adverse effect on air pollution or would we prefer to accept a smaller reduction in air pollution and at the same time hold down or reduce the cost of electric power and reduce our dependence on cartel controlled fuel oil from abroad? Should we seek to eliminate quickly all air pollution created by the automobile and bear the high cost in terms of emission controls or should we phase in the pollution controls over a longer time period and thus limit the cost increases for new cars?

Unfortunately, programs usually are presented in terms of the benefits to be derived while the costs are ignored or played down. Hence, we are not given a choice between meaningful alternatives. The bill is presented later, when it is almost impossible to reverse earlier decisions. Yet, a cost-benefit analysis is a vital prerequisite if we are to make intelligent decisions. This has been the key ingredient lacking in many social responsibility programs.

NOTES

1. Lee Loevinger, "Social Responsibility in a Democratic Society," in *Business Problems of the Seventies*, edited by Jules Backman (New York: New York University Press, 1973), p. 190.
2. See William Nordhaus and James Tobin, *Is Growth Obsolete?* (New York: National Bureau of Economic Research, 1972).
3. Roger M. Blough, former chairman of the board of United States Steel Corp., has emphasized that the performance of business in the economic area must be included in any evaluation of its "social performance." "Washington Encirclement of Business Decisions," The Benjamin Fairless Memorial Lectures (Pittsburgh: Carnegie-Mellon University, November 12, 1974), mimeograph, pp. 28–31.
4. According to *Business Week*, April 27, 1974, p. 63, there has been a very substantial increase in the percentage of annual reports that discuss some aspects of corporate social responsibility. See also *Report to Our Neighbors—1973* (New York: Citicorp, 1973), pp. 6, 7, 9, 14–15; and *Union Carbide Profile*, "Special Report: Social Progress" (New York: December 1974).
5. Milton Friedman, *New York Times Magazine*, September 13, 1970, pp. 33, 122–26.
6. "We need a new kind of social accounting that goes beyond GNP for the

nation and goes beyond net profit for the firm." Eli Goldston, *The Quantification of Concern* (Pittsburgh: Carnegie-Mellon University, 1971), p. 15.

7. John Diebold, *Financial Institutions and Social Priorities,* an address before the American Bankers Association, Chicago, Ill., October 9, 1973, p. 2.

8. *Economic Report of the President* (Washington, D.C.: Council of Economic Advisers, February 1974), p. 126.

9. Dow Chemical reported that in 1973 "554 pollution abatement projects were completed at a cost of $27 million," *1973 Dow Annual Report,* p. 18.

10. *Business Week,* May 13, 1972, p. 77, and June 8, 1974, p. 50c.

11. John E. Cremeans and Frank W. Segal, "National Expenditures for Pollution Abatement and Control," *Survey of Current Business* (February 1975), p. 9.

12. John R. Meyer, "Setting Environmental Standards: An Economist's View," *National Bureau Report,* Supplement (New York: National Bureau of Economic Research, May 1973), p. 3.

13. Nordhaus and Tobin, *op. cit.,* p. 24.

14. Eli Goldston has noted that "many proposed imprecise measures of social accounting can be sufficiently accurate to be instructive." Goldston, *op. cit.,* p. 15.

15. *Social Indicators, 1973* (Washington, D.C.: Office of Management and Budget, Statistical Policy Division, 1973), p. xiii.

16. David F. Linowes, *The Corporate Conscience* (New York: Hawthorn Books, 1974) Chaps. 5–7. See also Howard R. Bowen, *Social Responsibilities of the Businessman* (New York: Harper and Brothers, 1953), p. 156.

17. S. P. Sethi, "Corporate Social Audit: An Emerging Trend in Measuring Corporate Social Performance," in *The Corporate Dilemma: Traditional Values versus Contemporary Problems,* edited by Dow Votaw and S. P. Sethi (Englewood Cliffs, N.J.: Prentice-Hall, 1973), p. 219.

18. See Victor R. Fuchs, *Who Shall Live?* (New York: Basic Books, 1974), Chap. 3.

19. For a discussion of some of these points see Charles T. Stewart, Jr. and Corazon M. Siddayao, *Increasing the Supply of Medical Personnel* (Washington, D.C.: American Enterprise Institute, 1973), pp. 41–44, 50.

20. *New York Times,* April 18, 1975 and April 30, 1975.

21. Ford Foundation, *Annual Report* (1971), p. 92.

22. A Statement by the President and Fellows of Harvard College (Cambridge, Mass.: May 4, 1972).

23. John G. Simon, Charles W. Powers, and Jon P. Gunnemann, *The Ethical Investor* (New Haven, Conn.: Yale University Press, 1972), p. 1.

24. *Ibid.,* p. 56.

25. *New York Times,* June 27, 1974, p. 66.

26. John G. Simon, Charles W. Powers, and John P. Gunnemann, "A Prophylactic Portfolio?" *Foundation News* (New York: Council on Foundations, September/October 1972), p. 38.
27. Stefan H. Robock and Kenneth Simmonds, *International Business and Multinational Enterprises* (Homewood, Ill.: Richard D. Irwin, 1973), p. 149. See also *Social Responsibilities of Business Corporations* (New York: Committee for Economic Development, June 1971), p. 35.
28. Michael G. Duen, "International Business Management ... Its Four Tasks," in *The Multinational Enterprise in Transition,* edited by A. Kapoor and Phillip D. Gaubb (Princeton, N.J.: Darwin Press, 1972), p. 142; Helen Dinerman, "Image Problems for American Companies Abroad," in *The Corporation and Its Publics,* edited by John W. Riley, Jr. (New York: John Wiley, 1963), p. 141.
29. Raymond Vernon, "Multinational Enterprises in a World of National States: Performance and Accountability," in *Multinational Corporations, Trade and the Dollar,* edited by Jules Backman and Ernest Bloch (New York: New York University Press, 1974), p. 77.
30. *Ibid.,* p. 12.
31. For a comprehensive examination of the nature and magnitude of these costs see Murray L. Weidenbaum, *Government-Mandated Price Increases* (Washington, D.C.: American Enterprise Institute for Public Policy Research, February 1975).

TWO

Social Responsibility
of Organizations in
a Free Society

James M. Hester

President
New York University *

Social responsibility has become an extremely broad and deep subject. The most pertinent way in which I can address it is to emphasize those aspects with which I have had direct experience as a university president. My general topic is the social responsibility of organizations in a free society. Since the business corporation is the chief focus of discussions of social responsibility, I shall draw heavily on that example and point out parallels between it and the university whenever they are relevant to the general concept.

Our society has become increasingly concerned that greater affluence has not been accompanied by equal progress in solving important social problems. The latter include poverty, crime, drugs, and pollution of the environment. Though progress is now being made, there have been pressures building for more rapid and possibly radical

* On September 1, 1975 Dr. Hester became Rector of the United Nations University in Tokyo

shifts in the area of social responsibility. Growing criticism has developed with respect to those institutions, such as the corporation, that in the minds of some emphasize the maintenance of the status quo at the expense of social advances.

Today, the corporation is undergoing the most intensive public scrutiny in its history. Under the pressure of many forces, public and private, corporations have been increasingly enmeshed in controversy. It has been alleged that they are little concerned about the interests of the consumer, are indifferent to the deteriorating social order, and are dangerous polluters of the environment. As a result, according to a report of the Committee on Economic Development, "The public wants business to contribute a good deal more to achieving the goals of a good society. . . . Business enterprises, in effect, are being asked to contribute more to the quality of American life than just supplying quantities of goods and services." [1]

Unfortunately, there has been no general agreement as to the meaning of corporate social responsibility or how it should be implemented, despite the fact that many businessmen enthusiastically have adopted the concept during the past decade. Increasingly, corporate annual reports spell out a company's concern for social responsibility.

The literature on social responsibility is predominantly concerned with the business corporation, but in recent years the large university has been cited as an organization that also has social responsibilities beyond its traditional functions. Universities have come to share this distinction because they, too, have become large; they, too, appear to be successful and influential; and they, too, are possible sources of solutions to problems with which neither individuals nor government alone seem able to cope.

THE SOCIALLY RESPONSIBLE MANAGER

Irving Kristol, Henry R. Luce Professor of Urban Values at New York University, points out that this recognition has forced both corporate and university executives to alter their behavior. He writes:

Small business can still be single-minded in its pursuit of profitability, just as small colleges can still be single-minded in their
pursuit of education in the traditional way. But the large corporation, like the large university, impinges on too many people in
too drastic a way. And so the executives of the large corporation,
like the administrators of the large university, have to learn to
govern, not simply to execute or administer. And to govern is to
think politically, as well as economically or educationally. That is
the price of bigness and power.[2]

Professor Kristol is describing what the literature of business theory
refers to as the "socially responsible manager" as opposed to the manager motivated entirely by the maximization of profit. Professor
Thomas A. Petit, of the University of Arizona, a specialist in the
subject of social responsibility in business, gives the following description of this new managerial type:

The attitude of modern managers toward profit is markedly
different from that of the entrepreneur of yesteryear. The separa-
tion of ownership and control in the large corporation has given
managers a good deal of autonomy. They have been freed from
the necessity of pursuing profit single-mindedly in the stockholder's interest. Now they can emphasize other objectives such as
their own prestige; the leadership of the company in the industry;
and the welfare of employees, customers, and community. . . .
Many top managers behave as if they believe that they and their
companies are responsible for many of the social and political
problems of modern industrial society.[3]

Professor Peter Drucker, of New York University and Claremont
Graduate School, confirms this view:

Social responsibility cannot be evaded. It is not only that the
public demands it. It is not only that society needs it. The fact
remains that in modern society there is no other leadership group
but managers.[4]

Thus it seems that the apparent success of the corporation and the
university, coupled with disappointment with the problem-solving

capability of government, has encouraged the idea that these organizations must assume responsibilities beyond their traditional, specific functions. And, in both instances, leadership has often responded affirmatively. Many corporate and university spokesmen have declared themselves in favor of using the resources of their organizations for purposes far beyond their special functions. T. F. Bradshaw, president of the Atlantic Richfield Company, provides a striking example:

> The businessman does not exist solely in a world of cold, gray economics. He is a man before he is a businessman. He feels pressure from within himself to become a part of the whole social pattern and to accomplish more than making a profit. He also has pressures from without because, as a businessman, he is part of the power structure; and he must direct his portion of that power to accomplish some of the broader aims of the society in which he lives.[5]

Particularly since the crisis years of the 1960s, a principal reason for statements of this kind is the desire to use whatever talent and resources can be spared to help with problems whose solution seems essential to the viability of our society. As a result, traditional concepts of the appropriate functions of corporations and universities have been altered. Corporations and universities have been urged and, as the result of social and environmental legislation, have been required, to involve themselves in many activities far beyond their special functions. This is not a new experience for these organizations. It occurred during the First World War and again during the Second World War. In fact, it has become a normal response of American society to turn to the corporation and to the university, as its leading sources of talent and expertise, in times of crisis. Now that we live in an era in which new crises are constantly streaming toward us, it seems inevitable that increasing demands will be made on these organizations.

We are now in a period when ideas about the role of social responsibility are being reexamined rather critically. Changed economic circumstances are partly responsible. Some businesses and most universities are hard pressed to finance their basic functions. Business commitments to urban programs have been reduced. In universities, the economic crisis has superseded racial injustice as a focal issue and has forced a more pressing concern with issues fundamental to institutional survival. For example, the 1974 budget of the New York City Urban Coalition, which is supported largely by corporate gifts, was only one-third of the total five years ago.

There may also be some reaction against the full tide of social responsibility spending of the 1960s. Of course, given the short interest span of our society and its media, many causes lose attention and support, not because they are no longer thought important, but because other issues have stolen the limelight. New causes, such as pollution control and consumer safety, have moved into the priority position for many corporations under both public and governmental pressure. But also there is considerable disappointment with the results of some overambitious social programs undertaken during the sixties, and many executives, in both business and education, for reasons connected with both the economy and specific disappointments, are in a far more conservative mood today than they were then.

CRITICISM OF THE SOCIAL RESPONSIBILITY CONCEPT

In this climate, the opponents of the concept of social responsibility are getting a new hearing. Milton Friedman's views are more frequently discussed, and in higher education, such writers as Robert Nisbet, Schweitzer Professor at Columbia, have sounded a corresponding note. In his recent book, *The Degradation of the Academic Dogma,* Nisbet is highly critical of those tendencies that attempt to make the university "the capstone of the research establishment," "the microcosm of culture," "an adjunct to Establishment," "the radical critic of society," "humanitarian-in-chief," and "therapeutic community." [6] He argues that these tendencies have gravely weakened the American university by deflecting it from its fundamental functions of objective, detached scholarship and teaching.

There is an appealing quality to the arguments of writers like Friedman and Nisbet. They exhibit deep commitments to highly admirable objectives, such as political and economic freedom in the case of Friedman and teaching and scholarly excellence in the case of Nisbet. When consensus is lacking and convictions are wavering, strong, clear arguments in defense of strong, clear principles can have a tonic effect, whether or not after reflection they can be fully accepted.

In the academic world, critics of social responsibility are enjoying new popularity today because of multitudinous dissatisfactions with the condition of higher education. We are in a period of curricular uncertainty, and economic pressures have raised new questions about the role of the modern university. Perhaps a return to fundamentals, it is thought, would purge these institutions of distractions and of unnecessary baggage that have contributed to their instability. In the business world, critics of social responsibility are being heard anew, in part because of critical problems created by the energy crisis, the accelerating price inflation, and the recessionary economy.

In Professor Friedman's opinion, "there is one and only one social responsibility of business—to use its resources (for production) and engage in activities designed to increase its profits so long as it stays within the rules of the game." [7] Friedman views the market system both as the most efficient method of distributing resources and controlling costs and as the bulwark of economic and political freedom. He opposes the concept of social responsibility because it encourages interference in the functioning of the market system, causes irresponsible diversion of corporate resources from profits to social purposes, and results in dangerous meddling. He writes: "Few trends could so thoroughly undermine the very foundation of our free society as the acceptance by corporate officials of a social responsibility other than to make as much money for their stockholders as possible." [8]

In line with this view, Professor Theodore Levitt of Harvard has raised the specter of a "new feudalism," with the corporation investing itself "with all-embracing duties, obligations, and powers—ministering to the whole man and molding him and society in the image of the corporation's narrow ambitions and its essentially unsocial needs." [9]

DEFENSE OF THE SOCIAL RESPONSIBILITY CONCEPT

On the other hand, Professor Petit states:

The end of *laissez-faire* and the rise of the general welfare state have undermined the profit ethic by contradicting the basic assumption that the best individual and social result ensues when individuals pursue their self-interest in untrammeled freedom. The new dispensation emphasizes cooperation rather than competition, social interdependence rather than rugged individualism, and the human rather than the supernatural source of social and economic arrangements.[10]

Professor Petit perceives a "moral crisis in management" that is leading to "a turning point in business ethics because the inadequacy of the profit ethic is becoming clearly recognized." According to him, "an ideological and scientific foundation is being laid for the ethic of social responsibility," [11] which expresses the viewpoint of a group of businessmen, typified today by David Rockefeller, who, while a minority, are the leaders of the largest and most powerful corporations. He asserts that they are concerned, at least in part, that if they do not accept responsibilities commensurate with their power, they will lose their power "to someone antagonistic to business management and free enterprise." [12]

In part, this debate is futile because social responsibility means quite different things to different people. To some, being socially responsible means being honest, fair, and law-abiding. To others, these qualities are essential to good business, to sound long-range profit-making, and have nothing to do with the concept of social responsibility broadly conceived. To many businessmen social responsibility is closely related to good public relations and good corporate morale. Others would challenge assigning to social responsibility any activity that is a functional part of public or employee relations. Friedman argues that if a major industry in a community spends money on improving conditions in the community to enhance the quality of the labor it attracts, that is good business, not social responsibility:

> The crucial question for a corporation is not whether some action is in the interest of the corporation, but whether it is enough in its interest to justify the money spent. I think there will be many cases when activity of this kind will pay back dollar for dollar what the corporation spends. But then the corporation isn't exercising a social responsibility.[13]

If, as Friedman argues, the concept of social responsibility is both dangerous and disingenuous, why do serious men and women talk about it? Arjay Miller, former president of the Ford Motor Company and now dean of the Graduate School of Business at Stanford University, supplies an answer:

> The central fact of business today is that we are in a new ball game. We cannot return to the old, familiar ground rules. It is really not bad, in a way, that Adam Smith and Milton Friedman are not right. Life would be so much simpler if our task and our only responsibility was the narrow pursuit of profits.
>
> As it happens, tremendous new demands are being made on this society, and they in turn are causing tremendous new demands on business. . . . We should recognize that many of our most serious and urgent current demands are in the area of public, rather than private, goods. People want cleaner air and water, safer streets, less traffic congestion, better education systems, and so forth. These demands cannot be satisfied in the traditional market place.[14]

This, then, seems to be the rock bottom issue: are the over-riding problems of society so great, and the ability of the market mechanism and of governments to cope with them so inadequate, that for the sake of the general welfare, organizations whose obligations have been specific, limited functions, should allocate part of their energies and resources for public benefit? Obviously, an individual's response will reflect his views of the condition of society, the efficiency of market mechanisms, the effectiveness of government, and the competence of the institutions in question.

THE ROLE OF THE UNIVERSITY

The demands that might be made on the university are somewhat different from those made on businesses. Universities rarely produce profits or surpluses—deficits are far more typical. Except in cases of contributions to local governments in lieu of taxes in communities where they are the major user of services, it is seldom claimed that universities should make cash contributions to other organizations or causes. In fact, the legal conditions of much gift income would prohibit such contributions. Universities are, however, frequently invited to contribute services, all of which have costs. Thus, they find themselves being asked to divert resources away from teaching and scholarship to serve social values quite beyond their established functions. For example, a decade or more ago universities were frequently urged by federal agencies to undertake contracts to help institutions in developing countries as part of our national policy of foreign aid. There were many pressures both inside and outside universities to engage in these activities as part of a concept of international social responsibility.

Let me cite one illustration from an experience at New York University. In the early 1960s we accepted a federal contract to help establish the School of Administration in the University of Lagos in Nigeria. The monetary value of the time of New York University faculty and administrators invested in the project far exceeded compensation from the U.S. government. Thus, from its limited resources, New York University made a costly contribution to this U.S. government project. A few faculty members and administrators derived personal benefits from this experience, and the University had the satisfaction of making a useful contribution to a new university in a developing country. But the question can legitimately be raised: was this the appropriate use of New York University's limited resources? It has been suggested that such assignments should be handled by professional consultants rather than institutions that are hard-pressed to fulfill their obligations at home.

The answer to this question depends in part on one's perception of the role of the United States in foreign affairs and the relationship of American universities to the fulfillment of that role. In the early 1960s, when New York University undertook the Nigerian assignment, the cold war was still very hot. Particularly in Africa, the more developed nations were making substantial efforts to encourage the kinds of institutions they believed would lead to stable and progressive societies. To refuse to contribute when one had a special competency would have seemed both unpatriotic and anti-international.

In the era of domestic crises that followed the early 1960s, other kinds of requests were made of the University on behalf of the national interest. One striking example was a proposal from the Job Corps that New York University manage a job training school in the vicinity of Washington Square for girls from disadvantaged backgrounds. This program would have made use of some specialized expertise among a small number of faculty members in the School of Education, but its level of education was not that which the University traditionally provides. It was largely the University's potential management ability that was being sought. To have devoted the required amount of its limited management ability to this program woudl have constituted a considerable diversion of energies for the sake of social responsibility. This project did not develop at NYU, but the proposition was urged upon us.

During the same era, American universities became deeply concerned that they were not providing higher educational opportunities to a sufficient number of young people from disadvantaged minority groups. In order to address this problem, they undertook radical changes in their scholarship policies and added substantially to their scholarship budgets. New York University instituted one of the largest programs of this kind and in the years since has graduated far larger numbers of minority group students than it was ever able to do before. This has been an extremely costly endeavor, and it has contributed directly to the University's financial crisis. This is a typical example of a university undertaking a course of action in response to the concept of social responsibility.

Among the many books that have been published about universities in recent decades, relatively little has been written about their social responsibilities beyond those characterized as public service. In the triad of teaching, research, and public service, public service generally refers to such things as agricultural stations, adult education, and the hospitals and clinics that function as part of medical and dental education. The extensive research that has been undertaken largely with government funding, along with other public service or "humanitarian" activities, is part of what critics like Nisbet decry as detracting from truly academic functions. A very substantial part of government-sponsored research, however, has become integral to the teaching and basic research strength of our major universities. Without it they would not be as advanced scientifically as they are. It is a mistake, in my opinion, to look upon basic scientific research as an aspect of social responsibility apart from normal academic functions.

The whole of university activity, broadly conceived, is undertaken to meet needs of society; but narrowly conceived, the university exists to fulfill functions which are primarily of interest to academicians, the searchers after knowledge for its own sake. Seen this way, there are substantial similarities between profit and nonprofit institutions in respect to the concept of social responsibility. If the public service functions, including much research, of universities are viewed as diversions of resources from the essential functions of teaching and scholarship, it is possible to place them in a category similar to that of the nonprofit-related activities of business.

So the question becomes very much the same for both profit and nonprofit institutions in a free society. Should institutions concentrate their attention and energies entirely on their special functions or should they take a broader view of their responsibilities? Should corporations make unrestricted grants to universities, museums, orchestras, and hospitals? Should they contribute to minority worker training programs unrelated to their own labor supply? Should they finance minority businessmen? Should universities sponsor housing projects and provide services of its faculty staff to community projects not directly related to the well-being of the university itself? Should they concentrate on pure scholarship or concern themselves with the pressing problems of mankind?

SOME CONCLUSIONS

Having raised these questions, I should like to venture some answers to them.

My answers may offend theorists who analyze society and its institutions strictly in terms of their special functions and do not like their models contaminated with what seem to be dysfunctional and illogical relationships. But it is one thing to take positions in terms of theoretical models and another to seek to exert responsibility for preserving valuable institutions in a highly illogical, actual world.

My first argument for accepting the concept of the social responsibility [of organizations] is the recognition that our society is so beset by critical problems and so deficient in agencies for solving them that all capable individuals and organizations are obligated to undertake whatever responsibilities they can shoulder. That, of course, is a rather comprehensive assertion. It needs elaboration. Whether one is sympathetic to this point of view or not depends a lot on how one views trends in our society and whether anything can be done about them.

I perceive many highly destructive trends in our society, and I believe all of us with any influence should do our best to counteract them. I am concerned, for example, with the threatened decline of privately supported cultural and educational institutions, particularly if inflation continues its destructive course. Who can be counted on to help save the private organizations that give this city its intellectual and cultural quality, its attraction, and its vitality? Unless, in addition to whatever government agencies may do, we can count on vigorous corporate support, the effort to save these institutions will be futile. No corporations of which I am aware have deprived their employees or shareholders of significant income because of contributions for these purposes. Yet the aggregate of this support for an institution like NYU ($4 million annually) is absolutely crucial to our survival. Such gifts, in many instances, are not traceable to direct corporate benefits, but this city and nation would be far less attractive for all of us were this University and similar institutions unable to survive.

To repeat, it is the recognition of crucial social needs that will not be served in any other way that gives the concept of social responsibility its urgency. And this principle applies to nonprofit organizations as well as to businesses. A university must exercise strict discipline in allocating its resources to avoid both bankruptcy and mediocrity. But it cannot ignore the deterioration of the society around it and fail to make efforts it is qualified to undertake consistent with the fulfillment of its primary functions. Unless the leaders of all our major institutions are committed to the improvement of American society, I believe we face a gloomy future.

In arguing that the university must accept social responsibility, I do not suggest that it should assume managerial and other commitments which would detract from its ability to provide first-class teaching and research. The university's most important contributions to society are well-educated graduates and important new knowledge. But there are many ways in which teaching and research can be related to the crucial problems of society without forsaking high academic standards. It is not a distortion of the academic function to orient research and teaching toward the realities with which we must cope. Not every current issue deserves special emphasis in the university, but certainly such basic problems as race relations, urban planning, pollution, energy, population, and inflation warrant the concerted attention of the relevant academic disciplines.

We live in a time of profound challenge to all our institutions, including the university and the corporation. In my opinion these organizations need to do everything in their power to strengthen their credibility with the general public and with those who make public policy. Corporations and universities are not independent entities that can ignore their surroundings. They are creatures of law and can be seriously affected by what lawmakers and the voting public think of them. Therefore, for the sake of their own viability, it behooves these organizations to demonstrate public concern beyond their special interests.

My second argument for accepting the doctrine of social responsibility is, therefore, self-preservation. For a free society where the voters possess the freedom and the power to curb organizations whose policies they disapprove through the actions of their political representatives, it behooves organizations to be mindful of public attitudes and values.

It can be argued that what I am talking about is good public relations, which Professor Friedman would accept as a legitimate business or institutional expense. And there is no question that one man's social responsibility is another man's public relations. Where one ends and the other begins is hard to define, especially if you take the long view. But, certainly in the minds of management, there is a difference, and, ultimately, in the perceptions of the public, there is a difference. It behooves management, in my opinion, to strike a public posture that exhibits a responsible concern for the general welfare that clearly exceeds the limited interests of the organization. And in so doing corporate leaders would, in fact, be faithful to the views of Adam Smith himself. It should be remembered that in the *Theory of Moral Sentiments* he took the position that where the "wise and virtuous man" sees a choice between his private interest and the public good, he has a moral obligation to act to serve the public.[15]

An important consideration, I believe, is the attitudes that institutional leadership and policies encourage. Does the organization place a high priority on good citizenship, or does it not? Some do, notably. Some do not seem to care. Some corporations and universities encourage staff members to contribute time, energy, and moral support to public causes, and the effects are substantial. They account for a major part of the efforts that are made to sustain our voluntary hospitals, agencies, cultural organizations, and universities. This activity is unique to our kind of free society and one of its most admirable characteristics.

It is one of the great benefits of freedom to be able to make such contributions to the public good. This is a privilege for the individual, but it is also a privilege that organizations enjoy in our society. Organizations express the characteristics of their leaders who, in turn, are educated increasingly in universities. We have a responsibility here, therefore, to sensitize future organizational leaders to the socially responsible manner in which their influence can be used.

NOTES

1. *Social Responsibilities of Business Corporations* (New York: Committee for Economic Development, June 1971), p.15.
2. *The Wall Street Journal*, February 14, 1974.
3. Thomas A. Petit, *The Moral Crisis in Management* (New York: McGraw-Hill, 1967), p. 10.
4. Peter F. Drucker, *Management: Tasks, Responsibilities, and Practices* (New York: Harper and Row, 1973), p. 325.
5. T. F. Bradshaw, "Corporate Social Reform: An Executive's Viewpoint," *California Management Review*, Vol. 15 (Summer 1973), p. 86.
6. Robert Nisbet, *The Degradation of the Academic Dogma: The University in*

America, 1945–1970 (New York: Basic Books, 1971), Chap. 12, pp. 171–196.

7. Milton Friedman, *Capitalism and Freedom* (Chicago: The University of Chicago Press, 1962), p. 133.

8. *Ibid.*

9. Theodore Levitt, "The Dangers of Social Responsibility," *Harvard Business Review,* Vol. 36, No. 5 (September–October 1958), p. 44.

10. Petit, *op. cit.,* p. 12.

11. *Ibid.,* p. 13.

12. *Ibid.,* p. 8.

13. *Business and Society Review Innovation,* Spring 1972, p. 7.

14. Arjay Miller, "The Social Responsibility of Business," *A Look at Business in 1990* (Washington, D.C.: White House, Conference on the Industrial World Ahead, 1972), pp. 85–89.

15. Adam Smith, *The Theory of Moral Sentiments,* Vol. 2 (London: Strahan and Cadell, 1790), p. 115.

THREE

Who is Responsible for the Quality of Life?

Juanita M. Kreps

Vice-President

and

James B. Duke

Professor of Economics
Duke University

Disenchantment with American leadership had begun long before Watergate. Although it is too soon to measure the added fallout from that sequence of events, one conclusion is clear enough: confidence in most institutions, both public and private, has been declining sharply for some time.

The proportion of the public having "a great deal of confidence" in the executive branch of the government fell by more than a third (to about one in four respondents) between 1966 and 1973, according to Harris surveys. Congressmen and U.S. senators lost half their satisfied customers in the same period, again ending up with only about one in four people expressing strong confidence. Public regard for the Su-

preme Court took a similar slide, as it did for the military establishment. Outside government, equally severe losses appeared. Persons
with confidence in top business leaders dropped by half; for educators,
the decline was even more severe. Press and TV leaders, labor leaders,
and advertising heads (none of whom enjoyed a lot of popularity to
begin with) continued to lose supporters. Even physicians, who have
traditionally enjoyed high public esteem, lost one-third of their
advocates.[1]

The public's evaluation of business performance in specific areas is
revealing. More than half of the people think business is a "real help"
in building up the community, in backing scientific progress, and in
supporting higher education. But the corporate world gets very low
marks in controlling air and water pollution and in helping minorities
or needy groups. Meanwhile, the public's list of things business ought
to do is expanding. More than two-thirds of the people believe that
business should provide leadership in controlling pollution, rebuilding
cities, eliminating racial discrimination, and cutting down accidents
on highways. In addition to these social objectives, which are
frequently ascribed to corporations, the public now calls for corporate
leadership in an even longer list of concerns not traditionally considered the businessman's responsibility: eliminating depressions,
finding cures for disease, controlling crime, raising moral standards,
reducing the threat of war, raising living standards around the world
—even enabling people to use their talents creatively.[2]

Why the loss of public confidence in institutional leadership? Has
performance deteriorated markedly, or do we now merely have
documentation of a record which has been generally poor but easily
concealed? In view of their low rating, why does the public impute to
business a leadership role in a wide range of nonbusiness pursuits? The
final question, most worrisome of all: Are these current expectations
realistic?

RISING EXPECTATIONS AND
DECLINING PERFORMANCE

The impact of today's recession on corporate capacity to meet its generally accepted responsibilities should be kept clearly in mind, not because we are doomed to a continuation of current economic conditions, but because they illustrate the futility of shifting to the corporation responsibilities that have traditionally been assigned to the government. In particular, the expectation that business assume leadership in eliminating economic fluctuations (a goal in which the government has had only limited success) would seem unrealistic, given the state of knowledge as to how to reduce fluctuations and the constraints under which businesses operate. Moreover, concurrent inflation and recession underscore the extent to which corporations are falling short on their more modest objectives of raising productivity and lowering costs. Asking business firms to maintain stability in the economy is pointless; demanding that they improve productivity and thus lower costs is entirely appropriate. Drawing a distinction between the business system and the individual firm, Professor James McKie has noted:

> The system may fail to provide full employment, fail to innovate vigorously, fail to weed out the inefficient, fail to invite entrepreneurship, fail to respond to the needs of consumers, and may obviously fail to provide "public goods" and things that fall somewhat beyond its domain. Yet some of these "failings" represent expectations we should not have had in the first place, and others are aggregate failings rather than the shortcomings of individual firms.[3]

Disappointment with the performance of the business system (or the performance of a particular firm) is attributable in part to an overall rise in expectations that extends as well to nonbusiness institutions and to levels of personal achievement. The belief that governments can solve any social problem, and quickly, is widespread. John Gardner refers to a popular "vending-machine" concept of social betterment: Put in a problem and out comes a solution. If a ready remedy is not forthcoming, it is thought to be because someone in power is stupid or misguided, or both. We need to be reminded, Mr. Gardner argues, that some problems persist simply because we don't know how to solve them.[4] Similarly, higher education has been charged with a broadened mandate that extends to community affairs, the political process, and economic policy making, just at the time when the institutions' resource base began shrinking. It may be true that our expectations of personal relationships are equally unrealistic—that the high rate of divorce, for example, is related to the fact that through marriage one expects to enjoy a sense of security and fulfillment that marriage per se cannot guarantee. It is surely true that parents set unduly high standards for their children, and vice versa.

When one is disappointed in a personal relationship, frustration usually results, with bitterness sometimes ensuing. When the government fails to meet our standards, we vote the leadership out of office, assuming, of course, that our view of their performance is in the majority. In the case of business firms, there is no clear parallel; the action taken turns largely on who is disappointed. If the consumer is sufficiently dissatisfied, she stops buying the product. If the worker finds the job unsatisfactory, he or she may look for alternative employment. When stockholders lose money, they, too shift away from the firm. But "the public" that now demands that the corporation not pollute the air finds it more difficult to influence corporate behavior. Disenchantment with business policy has come increasingly from this group of people, and there is every sign that their protests will grow louder.

There is no evidence that disappointment with business performance is leading to lowered expectations; quite the contrary. As Howard Bowen indicates, the public's mood has changed dramatically in the last quarter-century: "To-day, economic efficiency, productivity, and growth—the staples of corporate enterprise—are valued less highly than they were twenty-two years ago."[5] He lists the current controversial list of demands: elimination of discrimination, improvement in the quality of work, observance of the law, protection of the environment, honesty in advertising and mass communication, reduced corporate influence on government and in international matters, reduced consumption of natural resources, and the development of a more equitable income distribution. And while the public views these as proper areas of corporate responsibility, Professor Bowen finds that few people believe corporations will voluntarily achieve the desired standards.[6] Hence the source of public cynicism: much is demanded but little is actually expected.

The current discrepancy between what business is charged with doing and what the public thinks it will actually do, given its necessary interest in the bottom line, fuels the debate on business morality.

> On the one hand, self-interested actions by businessmen are tolerated in law and approved in social mores. On the other hand, self-interest is considered to be an unworthy goal of action which conflicts with ethical norms to which society attaches great importance. This inconsistency creates ambivalence in social attitudes toward businesses . . .[7]

Such ambivalence and the cynicism it generates will continue to impede rational discourse as long as the public is encouraged to hold business responsible for activities that are not the proper domain of business. Granted that the corporations' social responsibility shifts through time—"What social responsibility requires today is what the law requires today plus what it will require tomorrow"[8]—there are nevertheless parameters which need to be specified if the notion of corporate responsibility is to assume any meaning whatsoever. Reasonable men will differ as to where to draw the line within a range of obligations, perhaps, but surely few would argue that business should provide special leadership in cutting out government red tape, worthy as that goal may be, or controlling population growth. Yet about half the people polled recently favored such leadership.

The basic question is this: Who is responsible for the quality of life? Should we hold institutions—governments, education, businesses—accountable for today's social ills, even as they claim credit for its advantages? Beyond the obvious requirement of observing the law, what ought to be the responsibilities of various social organizations? And once these responsibilities are assigned, how can we monitor and improve performance?

WHO SHOULD BE IN CHARGE OF WHAT?

Before specifying the dimensions of corporate responsibility, several prior questions must be addressed: questions of social goals, priorities, constraints, tradeoffs. If consensus can be reached on goals and priorities, if there is an understanding of the constraints imposed by resources and know-how, and if there is an acceptance of the terms of the tradeoffs involved in any choice among alternative courses of action, it is then possible to move to the question of who should be assigned various responsibilities. The process is not completed by imputing obligations to different institutions, however. It is meaningless to assign roles to institutions unless the institutions understand and accept the responsibilities or unless the law requires their acceptance. Legally required actions can scarcely be interpreted as evidence of "responsibility," since there is scarcely any choice, although "obedience to the unenforceable" [9] characterizes some regulatory areas. In order to gain voluntary compliance, means must be devised to persuade the corporation to accept the responsibility as a legitimate business activity. These issues can be summarized as three major questions:

- What do we want to have done?
- Who should do what? And who bears the cost?
- How do we institutionalize the assignments?

What Do We Want to Have Done?

Some of the current ambivalence on corporate roles is due to lack of clarity on social goals or, more precisely, an unwillingness to accept the costs of certain stated objectives, measured in terms of tax dollars or product prices, or in terms of other goods and services that would have to be forgone. Although our concern here is with the question of which social obligations are properly assigned to business, prior questions of society's goals and priorities—how they are set and perceived by the public—must be examined.

The process of setting social goals through elected representatives has popular endorsement; yet the performance of those selected by this process has seldom been under such severe attack. Indeed, even businessmen and educators now fare better in the public eye, perhaps because

> It has been the government—not business—that has made the great decisions on war and peace, on crime and punishment, on educational patterns and methods, on expenditures for armaments, as opposed to welfare or health care, on tax and monetary policy, and on many other matters that are the cause of bitter debate.[10]

In light of these bitter debates, it is often difficult to interpret the wishes of the electorate. Was the election of a Democratic Congress a mandate to spend heavily in order to combat unemployment, as opposed to minimizing the budget imbalance in the interest of containing inflation? Or was it merely a vote against the previous president?

Interpretation of the voters' wishes is made, nevertheless, and societal goals do emerge in the form of legislative and administrative action. Priorities come to be established: Reducing unemployment takes precedence over a balanced budget and anti-inflation measures; energy needs are to be met at the expense of some lowering of environmental standards; tax rebates are aimed at stimulating spending, in contrast to the tax increase proposed a year or so earlier, etc. Public understanding of these measures is limited, unfortunately, and the necessary tradeoffs are seldom accepted. For example, the tight-money policy that was used to fight inflation dampened the construction of new homes and lowered the number of jobs in that industry. Lack of labor support for this policy is, therefore, not surprising. Or take another area: What are reasonable environmental standards in the face of energy shortage?

Just as clarity of social objectives is difficult to achieve, so, too, is the vision necessary to invent a better future. In retrospect, the errors in judgment are quite easy to identify. Throughout the last half of the nineteenth and the first seven decades of the twentieth century, governments encouraged a rapid growth in those industries which today threaten the environment. Loevinger reminds us:

The automobile was hailed in the beginning as much for the fact that it would eliminate horses, and their ubiquitous soiling of the streets, as for the convenience it offered in transportation. This was regarded as a cleansing of the environment. . . . The simple fact is that yesterday nobody foresaw the consequences that today are plain to everybody.[11]

In a similar vein, Arthur Schlesinger, Jr., has pointed out that social progress itself creates new problems:

Improved methods of medical care and nutrition have produced the population crisis; and the growth and redistribution of population have produced the urban crisis. The feverish increase in the Gross National Product first consumes precious natural resources and then discharges filth and poison into water and air. Hence the ecological crisis.[12]

These reminders illustrate the difficulties in agreeing on what it is we want to do. The further question of who assumes the obligation of seeing that objectives are met needs to be distinguished, in turn, from the issue of who bears the cost of various services. Debate over corporate responsibility continues to confuse the two questions, despite a vast literature on externalities.

Who Should Do What, and Who Pays?

Consider, for example, the case of air pollution. Producers of goods which contribute to this problem traditionally have failed to accept responsibility for undoing the damage generated in the production process or in the subsequent use of the goods. And since neither business nor anyone else assumed leadership, true pollution costs, measured in terms of a deteriorating environment, have been borne by the entire public rather than being charged to the users of the product. Alternatively, the producer could now take the position that the full cost of the good, including the cost of meeting all environmental standards, should be charged to the purchaser. If these costs make the product prohibitively expensive, sales will fall and ultimately, perhaps, the good will go off the market. Pollution from that source is then eliminated by restricting production and sales to those customers who are willing to pay full costs.

But suppose the good is vital to the livelihood of consumers, including those who have low incomes. Electric power comes quickly to mind. Subsidies also come to mind. Tax revenues can be used to keep down the cost of utilities to these consumers, either by providing income supplements to low-income families or by subsidizing the cost of anti-pollution measures directly. In either case, the cost of cleaner air is borne by taxpayers, presumably those of middle- and high-income levels.

Some portion of the cost of anti-pollution measures can of course be paid from profits. The impact of higher costs and reduced returns to owners of capital will vary, depending on alternative outlets for investment. In the case of some utility companies, severe cutbacks in growth already have resulted, and threats of power shortages are always with us. Reductions in energy consumption obviously are called for, and measures designed to bring about the lifestyle changes that would lead to such decreases are absolutely essential. In the interim, the person who pays for an improvement in the environmental condition is the consumer, or the taxpayer, or the investor; the result, in any case, is a shift from private goods to public goods consumption, and probably some redistribution of real income.

What ought to be the corporation's role in making this shift? Should business lead the way in directing the use of resources toward societal goals, insofar as there is consensus on these goals? Or is the leadership role better assumed by public bodies and by the consumer? If in achieving a particular objective the cost is charged in such a way as to bring about some redistribution in favor of the low-income groups, what is the corporate obligation?

To take a more direct example: If four out of five people believe that business should take the lead in wiping out poverty, what ought to be the corporate response?

The response from business, if it were polled, would probably be cautious but not necessarily negative. Caution might argue that the process of wiping out poverty would take time, that the costs to the nonpoor should not be overlooked, that certain institutions (education, for example) would need changing. But for the most part business leaders might argue that, to the extent they are successful in increasing the nation's output, they are making poverty unnecessary. They might further argue that any redistribution of aggregate output should be achieved through taxation and spending by governments rather than by corporate action.

When the questions become more specific, the responses become more meaningful. Should corporations develop training programs, particularly for minorities? Undoubtedly. Do they have responsibilities for providing fringe benefits, notably for nonworking periods, through disability, supplementary unemployment benefits, and adequate pensions? These can no longer be in question. Should they guarantee nondiscriminatory hiring and promotion policies? Of course. Corporate policies in these areas are less likely to lag behind public opinion, particularly in periods of relatively full employment when competition for labor is strong. But legislation gets the credit for recent antidiscriminatory policies throughout the industry, and employee pressure accounts for many of the fringe benefits. Corporations have often participated only reluctantly in moves to improve the worker's status.[13]

The view that business should lead in the formation and pursuit of societal goals, in addition to tending its own affairs, is perhaps a tribute to that sector. Business has its own problems under control, it argues, and can now assume additional functions. But even if it were possible for business to shift its attention away from the management of business affairs, does it follow that the corporation is particularly well equipped to interpret the public's wishes and to direct the allocation of resources into socially desirable projects? Beyond responding to consumer preference expressed in the marketplace and public sentiment expressed in governmental directive, which sets of signals is business to answer? If environmentalists argue for cleaner air and consumers for more fuel, is there any resolution except by democratic vote? In a period of job layoffs, when either seniority rules or the maintenance of jobs for minorities, but not both, can be honored, the choice should surely not be exclusively management's. Indeed, there is a curious contradiction in the insistence on corporate responsibility for social programs at a time when diffusion of decision-making authority is itself a highly sought objective.

The division of social responsibility among various institutions and groups of people shifts through time, if for no other reason than the fact that new obligations appear and they must be assumed by someone. Arrangements that served the needs of a less complex society no longer are adequate today.

Consider one example. Until fairly recently, the care of older people was provided altogether within the family. Man's work, which was largely in the agricultural sector, continued through most of his life, and, since the proportion of the population surviving to old age was low, the burden of supporting retirees was minimal. At the present time, however, practically all babies born in this country will survive to maturity, and the length of time each succeeding generation spends in retirement is growing. The institution through which financial and living arrangements were made in the past—the family—has passed its obligations on to the government, private pension arrangements, retirement communities and homes, and a fairly elaborate system of medical care.

In retrospect, was the corporate response to this emerging social need adequate? Should a business firm's responsibility for the maintenance of income for the elderly extend beyond its present commitment for pensions of its own employees? The government assumed the task of developing a system that builds a floor of income and basic medical care for all retirees, some would say, perhaps, because industry failed to do so.

How Can We Institutionalize the Assignments?

The question of who should respond to each new social problem ought to be resolved, ultimately, on the basis of which institution is best able to respond, or can develop the capacity to do so while continuing to perform its primary function—assuming, of course, that its function needs to be performed. In imputing to corporations a new responsibility, it is therefore necessary to consider whether the social obligation is one that is consonant with the overall objectives of business, or whether conflicts will ensue. If corporate acceptance of the new role compromises the corporate function, then one of two conclusions is inevitable: Either the social responsibility, although nominally accepted, will not actually be discharged by business nor, quite possibly, by any other institution; or the corporation becomes a somewhat different institution, willing to pursue objectives that may or may not be in the best interest of the company, its owners and employees.

Emphasizing the importance of long-run goals, under which many actions can be justified as profitable and therefore acceptable to corporations, does not resolve the question. The long run has generally been a consideration in corporate planning, although the ability to foretell future events is as limited in the business community as elsewhere. Neither short-run profit maximization nor maximization of profits in the long run, for that matter, is a requisite for corporate integrity. But profits are required if the firm is to continue in existence (unless incentives other than profits can be substituted), and the profit must be high enough to attract the necessary capital. Businesses cannot promise to place their social responsibilities above this degree of profitability except at their own peril. As Professors Cohen and Cyert have noted:

> There may be a conflict for some firms between pollution control and profit. This conflict becomes particularly strong when the society has not passed the appropriate laws which embody its social values and the corporation is left with the problem of voluntarily reducing its profit in order to contribute to some social goal.[14]

Other conflicts may arise, since corporations, like governments, have multiple goals. The corporate goals of producing a larger volume and the social goal of distributing the product in a particular fashion may sometimes conflict. Transfers of income to nonworking groups, for example, may direct funds into current consumption when business would prefer to have the money spent on capital goods. Traditionally, we have espoused the right of business to increase its output as long as demand sustained such growth. But we have not until very recently imputed to business any responsibility for deciding how the total product should be apportioned. The pricing mechanism has rationed the output among persons willing and able to pay for it, and the ability to pay depended in turn on the productivity and earnings of the buyer. As growth raised earnings in general, purchasing power rose and goods were dispersed among the working population.

Insofar as the allocation of total product was influenced by non-market forces, the influence has been exerted through governmental action in the form of taxes, subsidies, regulation of wages, and public spending in general. It was public sentiment translated into government action that eliminated child labor, set minimum wages, approved tax support for education, established public pensions and unemployment insurance—measures that have had a marked effect on the distribution of income. Throughout the nation's economic evolution, during which these social requirements were set, there has been no apparent expectation that business, rather than the legislatures, should be the group which instigated such social change. On the contrary, in these instances business has had to be instructed by governments to behave in ways that contravened the dictates of the market.

What is different today is not that people are suddenly demanding actions of business, whereas in the past business was free to respond only to market forces. Business has always been obligated to observe the rules laid down by the public's elected representatives. Rather, the difference lies in the degree to which business is now asked to interpret the public's preferences, even before governmental action has stipulated what should be done. Corporations are under attack for failing to adopt antipollution measures before the law required that they do so; for waiting to have affirmative action rules laid down by government, rather than announcing such plans voluntarily; for not lobbying for antipoverty measures and worker safety and intelligent resource use.

The question of institutionalizing such a broad range of responsibilities is perhaps premature, since there is not yet a consensus on which ones properly beong to the corporation. It is clearly true, nevertheless, that businesses today are accepting obligations not previously thought to be in their domain. It is further true, as Professor McKie has argued, that the business system can do many things that the individual firm cannot do. And it is of course the business system that is being challenged to find ways to solve social problems, some of which it has helped to create. If businesses as a group are to respond effectively to this challenge, they must be willing to take actions that are not necessarily in their best collective short-run interest. Such actions are plagued with many problems: uncertainty even as to long run return; the "free-rider" who gains from improvement in conditions without bearing any of the costs; [15] most of all, perhaps, an inability to achieve businesswide agreement on courses of action. In view of these difficulties, it is not surprising that business looks to government for assurance that the same guidelines apply to all firms.

Incentives to corporations to take action which they would not otherwise initiate take several forms: pressure from consumers, employees, or the public generally; profit incentives; governmental regulation—all these means can be employed to bring acceptance and, eventually, the institutionalization of a wider mandate to businesses. Many analysts, however, do not expect a sudden expansion in the social responsibilities corporations will voluntarily undertake. The authors of one recent study come to this conclusion:

> As long as the business firm remains an essentially private organization, distinct from the state and with private ownership essentially intact, it cannot accept responsibility for problems that lie any appreciable distance outside its traditional economic concerns. [16]

GOVERNMENT, BUSINESS, AND THE SPECIAL CASE OF ENERGY

But "appreciable distance" is a flexible term and many corporate executives have endorsed some expansion in their activities. There is an important leadership role that is not incompatible with business objectives. The president of the Exxon Company has noted: "today's large corporation is responsive to broad social goals because it is managed for the long run." [17] An executive of Western Electric stated: "The Company will apply its business and management expertise to the selection, planning, and implementation of social action." [18] In a long look at the future, Neil H. Jacoby predicts that by 1990 business managers will be heavily committed to their social obligations. The profit motive notwithstanding, he argues, management will be judged as much by their ability to respond to public demands as by their profit records. He has words of comfort, too, for today's harassed corporate executive:

> By the last decade of this century, the strident criticism of business . . . will have abated. Large companies will have become sensitive to changes in the values of the public . . . and will have equipped themselves to sense and respond rapidly to those values. Also, the public will have come to understand the need to provide incentives for business participation in social activities, and the government will provide them.[19]

These incentives will take the form of direct contracts that hire businesses to do many of the things the public would now assign to them: train and educate, rebuild slums, deliver health care, build urban transportation, provide police and fire protection. In the "social-industrial complex" the partnership will be successful because it will utilize business talents to meet social demands directly and presumably profitably.[20]

While this collaboration with the government would resolve many of the potential conflicts corporations face in meeting the social demands being imputed to them in today's context, the larger question of how to shift the necessary resources into such social endeavors, and out of private consumption, is still with us. As social goals shift, so, too, must expenditure patterns; otherwise, the old goals continue to prevail. If performance is to be consonant with new social priorities, these priorities must come to be reflected in the way in which business and consumers behave—particularly in their response to the emerging shortages of food and energy.

In the case of energy, patterns of consumption in the richer nations have already begun to reflect the limitations on world supply. But these minor adjustments will have to be superseded by far greater cutbacks if we are to stretch limited resources far enough into the future to allow for the development of alternative sources. During the next two decades, while society is searching for ways to reduce consumption and increase the production of energy, important changes in lifestyle will be necessary.

In an era of extreme shortage, freedom of action is often necessarily restricted. Just as consumer choice will be limited by the energy supply, so, too, will the range of corporate activity and the rate of economic growth. A focus on future constraints—near the long-term—may place some current questions in different perspective. Consumers will not be able to command cheap fuels and, having to spend a larger portion of their incomes for gas and electricity, their levels of living will not rise but may even decline. Corporate expansion may be restricted, not only because demand is slowed, but also because the fuel available to them is expensive or nonexistent. The government will surely extend its regulatory authority over business, leaving a somewhat narrower range for voluntary corporate action.

The magnitude of these issues would seem to outweigh many questions now being debated under the rubric of corporate responsibility. What is called for is a constructive business response to an acute social problem that business has not faced heretofore: limited resource supply. And whereas the usual business response to short supply is to produce more, in this instance corporations may have to be content to produce less—at least until new sources of energy are developed. Given today's dilemma, evidence of concern about energy supplies for the future would be the best proof that corporations are farsighted, and perhaps the best assurance that they and the society will have a future.

Distinguishing between the responsibility of the business establishment and that of the government in the development of an energy program is difficult. In line with Jacoby's reasoning that business can be counted upon to produce the social goods society calls for when the government provides the proper incentives, it would follow that governmental guidelines should insure the promise of sufficient profits to induce business to find new energy supplies. Similarly, governmental policy should lead consumers to lower their use of energy. John Diebold offers further support of this view. Rather than making social decisions, he argues, "The businessman should be the tool who responds to market demand by making what society shows it wants. Do not make him more mighty than that." [21]

One of the major problems inherent in establishing a national energy policy is that of deciding what constitutes "sufficient profits." The public's reaction to the profits earned by the major oil companies during the period of the energy crisis reveals a wide discrepancy between the level of return the industry thinks necessary and the level acceptable to the public. Unless the corporations can persuade the public that industry profits are not rising more rapidly than other shares; that "over the past 20 years or so the rewards going to the corporate sector in the form of before-tax profits have declined from 16 percent to 11 percent of the national income, while rewards to corporate employees in wages and salaries have gone up," [22] public confidence in the social conscience of business will remain low.

The debate on profit margins not withstanding, the major challenge before corporations today is that of finding ways to meet the world's critical energy needs. A national energy policy laid down by the government will merely provide a framework which industry and the consumers will then have to implement. Leadership, not only in developing new sources, but also in conserving existing supplies, need not make the corporation into an all-purpose institution that attempts to right all social wrongs.[23] On the contrary, the business system is now the only institution capable of calling together the resources necessary to meet the challenge.

I conclude with this worry over the corporation's responsibility in the energy field, because energy is clearly our next Waterloo. Environmental concerns will of course continue, and will inevitably conflict with the pressure to increase energy supplies. What business does in this area in which there is no clear consensus is something of a test case.

We may legitimately call on industry to use its expertise to develop energy sources. We may not, I think, thrust onto the corporate world the decision as to how resources ought to be allocated as between antipollution or energy production. This decision ought to be made with some care by each of us, either through the voting process or by the force of our consumer demand. If we impute the responsibility to business, we may give up far more in freedom of choice than we gain, temporarily, in freedom from daily vigilance.

NOTES

1. From Harris Surveys, as published in *Public Attitudes Toward Business* (New York: Institute of Life Insurance, March 1974).
2. *Ibid.*, Exhibits 11 and 12.
3. James W. McKie, *Social Responsibility and the Business Predicament* (Washington, D.C.: The Brookings Institution, 1975), p. 4.

4. John Gardner, *No Easy Victories* (New York: Harper and Row, 1968), p. 28.

5. Howard R. Bowen, "Social Responsibility of the Businessman—Twenty Years Later," (1975) Mimeographed. See also his *Social Responsibilities of the Businessman* (New York: Harper and Brothers, 1953).

6. *Ibid.*

7. Francis X. Sutton, *The American Business Creed* (Cambridge, Mass.: Harvard University Press, 1956), pp. 354–355.

8. Lee Loevinger, "Social Responsibility in a Democratic Society," in *Business Problems of the Seventies,* edited by Jules Backman (New York: New York University Press, 1973), p. 178.

9. See James A. Wilson, "The Politics of Regulation," in McKie, *op. cit.,* pp. 135–168.

10. Loevinger, *op. cit.,* p. 186.

11. *Ibid.,* pp. 184–185.

12. Arthur Schlesinger, Jr., "The Velocity of History," *Newsweek* (July 7, 1970), pp. 33–34.

13. See Charles Myers, "Management and the Employee," in McKie, *op. cit.,* pp. 311–350.

14. Kalman J. Cohen and Richard M. Cyert, "Strategy: Formulation, Implementation, and Monitoring," *The Journal of Business of the University of Chicago,* Vol. 46 (July, 1973), p. 351.

15. McKie, *op. cit.,* p. 10.

16. See articles by Marvin A. Chirelstein, Thomas C. Schelling, Roland N. McKean, James O. Wilson, Martin Bronfenbrenner, Jerome Rothenberg, John F. Kain, Benjamin Chinitz, Raymond Vernon, Charles A. Myers, and James W. McKie in McKie, *op. cit.*

17. Randall Myer, "The Role of Big Business in Achieving National Goals," in an address given November 26, 1974.

18. D. K. Conover, "Corporate Social Responsibility," in an address given January 18, 1974.

19. Neil H. Jacoby, *Corporate Power and Social Responsibility* (New York: Macmillan, 1973), pp. 260–261.

20. *Ibid.,* p. 257.

21. John Diebold, *The Social Responsibility of Business,* an address given in Paris, June 21, 1972, p. 3.

22. Meyer, *op. cit.,* p. 8.

23. Diebold, *op. cit.,* p. 3.

FOUR

Does GNP Measure Growth
and Welfare?

Oskar Morgenstern

Professor of Economics
New York University

The question posed by the title of this paper raises a number of deep problems of economic science. The question seems simple, yet in these few words—measurement, growth, welfare—culminate the problems of large areas with which economists have been concerned for centuries. How nice it would be if one could report that now we have one single concept and, indeed, one single number which could summarize variations of growth and welfare. As we shall see, this unfortunately is not the case.

THE PROBLEM OF MEASUREMENT

All sciences have to come to grips with the problem of measurement. It is an extremely difficult one and each science has its own troubles. When a measurement in any field has become possible this is rightly hailed as a great achievement, as a step forward toward new discoveries and innumerable applications. Even to have a precise measure of time is difficult. Clocks are a late development in human history, and to this day we try to make them more and more accurate because so much depends on them. So it is not surprising that, when it was recently reported, the rotation of the earth—our finest measure of time—may have slowed down during the last year by one second, this caused great interest in physics and astronomy. From this reaction we also get an idea of the high standards in those sciences. In other fields we measure blood pressure, barometric pressure, the composition of blood, temperature, the speed of light, etc., sometimes crudely, sometimes with extraordinary precision.

Although in the physical and even in the biological sciences a great and firm tradition has built up over the centuries, the matter of observation and measurement is never closed. Science is never finished; rather, for all time, science is only an approximation of the underlying reality. It may surprise you that in spite of this great tradition Einstein, as he more than once remarked to me, said: "Most scientists naively think they know what they should observe and how they should measure it." And he had the natural sciences in mind!

What then is the situation in the social sciences, in particular economics? In some manner we seem to be more fortunate than the natural sciences. Nature shows itself to our senses essentially in a qualitative way and to get to numbers of high precision requires great effort and is a formidable achievement. But in economics we can count, for example, the number of inhabitants of a town or of a country, the number of motor cars, of checks cashed, of tons of steel produced, of . . . well almost anything—or so it seems. Since it seems to be so simple to observe and to count, there is in economics—as well as in other social sciences—no tradition which would enforce high standards. Counting seems natural and what is counted is readily accepted. But that is true only up to the point where broader notions are encountered, such as "growth" and "welfare."

Or even more basic, the question of what are "value" and "utility" causes great difficulty. Suddenly we see that we must have sharp concepts, that we must ask questions to which we normally get only qualitative, not quantitative, answers. There is little doubt what an individual is, or what a motor car, a check, or other such recognizable item is. But to observe "growth" or "utility" or "welfare" for a whole nation is an entirely different matter. Surely people are involved, and cars that can be counted, or monies changing hands, and so on. But to state how the economy grows and whether welfare changes and by how much are entirely different matters. They ought to be approached with caution, respect, indeed with trepidation.

When we mention such words we know that they mean very different things to different people. In fact, for many they may mean nothing concrete or tangible. They are abstractions, possibly of a high order. We feel that there is some reality touched, but we also know that it is a long way from the state of affairs to truly scientific objective knowledge. What we need in order to observe, and hopefully to measure, are concepts. There is no escape from that. No matter how primitive our approach may be, a concept is involved. Good, useful concepts are hard to come by.

THE NATURE OF GROWTH

Let us first look at "growth." That is clearly a notion that applies to an organism. The human body grows, stops growing, and eventually dies. The body has many parts and many functions. It grows not only as a whole, but parts of it grow at different rates and not forever as already analyzed by Galileo. The whole is of unimaginable complexity which modern biology reveals to us in a rapid though still partial manner. In the whole process of organic growth there is control, genetic planning, and unified function. Can the economy be compared with this so that we could transfer the notion of organic growth from this area to our field? One thing is certain: The economy is also of the highest complexity. Consequently, one must expect that even an adequate qualitative description is correspondingly difficult.

I find, however, that very few men, even few economists, or should I say regretfully, especially economists, have a real appreciation and understanding of the immense complexity of an economic system. Now I have used the word "system" but it is not even clear whether the word "system" is appropriate because we do not understand fully the organizing principles that make the economic life of a nation possible.

One need only observe what happens in an ordinary person's day and what is considered to be absolutely obvious and normal. We take a bus in the morning, we take a train, we go to stores, we buy, the money with which we pay is accepted, or we pay by a check which will be presented to an anonymous institution, possibly far away, transmitted by mails over which we have no control whatsoever. The stores order and have things in stock, they set prices on the basis of the expectation of what competitors might be doing, we are buying on the same basis of expectation as to what our needs might be in the future and how they will be met, we spend our money today because we expect that our salaries or incomes from other sources actually will be paid at certain dates in the near or more distant future, etc.

In all this, there is no central genetic regulation, no double Helix, nobody who plans for all; there is no one to whom everybody is responsible. We carry a great deal of information in our heads, and that which we do not carry we can find in newspapers which gather information and are printed, again motivated only by their own self-interest, namely, to write, to publish, and to sell with profit. At present, at this very moment, raw materials are being produced, for which there is no conceivable way of telling how they will finally be molded, into which kind of finished products they will be turned. A steel producer has only the roughest idea whether his raw steel will be used for the making of tanks, of ships, or of paper clips.

And yet all this works and works miraculously well, although of course it is easily subject to great disturbances. The astonishing fact is not that the thing does not work well, but that it works at all. It is only when we realize the complexity of the economy that we begin to see, and possibly understand, how dangerous it is to interfere in these matters. The economic system, in addition, is subject to great changes, caused partly by technology, partly by strictly political events, and partly by changes in the desires and wishes of the final consumers. There is thus more than one uncertainty element which governs everything.

The human body, or any living organism, is in many ways a very much simpler matter. However, one who knows anything at all about the body's physiology would find this statement horrendous, because one can hardly imagine anything more finely tuned and more complicated than, let us say, the human body, not to mention the brain which is, without any doubt, the most complicated device of whose existence we are aware in the whole universe, and whose function we clearly do not fully understand, although we have a tremendous amount of knowledge of it. The fact is that the human body has one unique process, namely to stay functioning, and to stay alive. We cannot say that the economic system has any such clear purpose.

In the light of such observations, one should become extremely modest in making proposals for policy. In general, I would say that unless we are reasonably sure that we know what the consequences of new policy measures will be—for example, of new taxes introduced, prices regulated, etc.—we should leave things alone. One interferes only if one believes that one understands what the consequences of the interferences are. The same is true of medicine: It took a long time to come from the witch doctor to the modern brain surgeon. While presumably the human physiology, or that of any animal or any other biological entity, stays practically the same throughout centuries or millennia—although subject to evolution over hundreds of thousands of years—the economic system, to make things still more difficult, is constantly being changed, especially by technology.

Technology is an interference from the outside. It is absorbed in a manner which those who bring it into economic existence think to be profitable for them to do but whose global effects they neither understand nor care about. Clearly, this compounds the difficulties of policy, because what might have been a suitable measure to achieve desired results at one time may no longer have any validity under present or future circumstances. It takes a long time to develop a scientifically acceptable new idea of policy, and while it is being born—if that happens at all—new features appear in economic life. For example, Keynesian policy ideas of the 1930s are now being adopted by the U.S. government at a time when they have virtually no applicability whatsoever.

Thus, the "growth" of an economy is a very different matter from the growth of an organism. The economy has neither a beginning nor an end. In addition, as already said, the economy certainly changes. So it is perhaps not surprising that apart from some highly technical and abstract models of economic expansion—which is not the same thing as growth—there simply does not exist a generally accepted scientific concept which would give us the basis for a reliable numerical measurement of the *rate* of growth.

LIMITATIONS OF GNP

But there is GNP, gross national product, i.e., the turnover in an economy in a unit period, a hallowed notion in contemporary economics. It is used with abandon. I shall say more about it later. Now I want to point out only *one* of its quantitative features: It is expressed by a *single* number, a so-called scalar. We discussed organic growth of, say, a human body. Would anybody in his senses imagine that there could be a single scalar number which would adequately describe the development of a human from babyhood to maturity to old age: the growth of the body, of the mind, of capabilities? The idea is so grotesque and ludicrous that we can dismiss it from the outset.

We have just seen that the economy, too, is of high complexity and therefore that its description, or rather its changes, could be given and measured—accurately, without the slightest error of measurement!—by one scalar number is equally absurd. If one could design a method whereby changes are at least recorded by a vector—i.e., a number that has many components—it could be a different matter. I know of no such effort. Of course a "vector" is a more sophisticated concept and would not be useful for the simple and trivial interpretations which the single scalar unit makes so easy. Just to show the absurdity and limitation of this popular alleged "concept" consider the following.

Anything that leads to a transaction in monetary form, where goods and services change hands for money, is recorded as *positive*. No matter what is being sold, it enters GNP. It may have been sales of goods already stocked, it may have been a car just coming out of a factory: It does not matter. Neither does it matter *what* it is: Atomic bombs, drugs, cars, food, aesthetic pollution by new billboards—you name it. Clearly, that goes against common sense. Why should all products and services be treated alike? If I do not like more nuclear weapons, why should I accept a measurement that includes them as part of the "growth" of the economy? Of course, one could argue that one is only interested in *transactions*. But then one would have a great deal of explaining to do as to how more mere transactions can possibly be related to "welfare." Does the uncontrolled increase of cancer cells in a child mean "growth"?

There are other equally well-known difficulties. Many services are rendered and many goods are produced that never enter a market. Thus they escape GNP. As has been noted by many, if housewives were being paid by their husbands, GNP would rise, although there would not be one iota of difference in production or services. There are many other similar situations.

Another trouble with the GNP concept is that it measures, or rather expresses, as *positive* the *malfunctions* of the economic system or society. To wit: If we are stuck in one of the thousands of traffic jams, if airplanes are stacked and cannot land on schedule, if fire breaks out and other disasters occur that require repair—*up goes the GNP*. More gasoline is used, fares go up, overtime has to be paid, and so on. It would be difficult in any other science to find a "measure" which tells simultaneously opposite stories of the functioning of a complex system in *one* single scalar number! If we merely improve the scheduling of airplanes and stagger the times of automobile traffic, and nothing else is changed—*down goes GNP!* It goes *up*, on the other hand, if industry pollutes the air and we create other industries which remove the polluting substances.

So we see that there is real trouble with the basic underlying notion of GNP. It is not an acceptable scientific concept for the purposes for which it is used. The fact that it violates common sense might be considered not too critical. There are, after all, many concepts in physics which common sense would never create or judge, or might reject—such as, for example, "curved space." But these concepts are the product of powerful theories and are needed when a scientific field is already well developed. But the GNP is nothing of this kind. It expresses a trivial idea which is clearly accessible to scrutiny by common sense. Therefore, its current, indiscriminate uses are suspect and it is certainly questionable that it should be used to tell us about growth and welfare.

At this point, it is proper to recall Einstein's remark that it seems obvious to many what one should observe. Surely transactions occur all the time in the economy, but that does not mean that they offer the proper way to describe the functioning of the economy. Perhaps only *some* transactions may give us the desired information, only a selection made on the basis of a powerful theory. But what we see is that the corrections—or rather changes—of GNP figures that are made by elimination of the effect of seasonal variations, of price changes, etc., in no way touch the fundamental issues and objections.

GNP is a *global* notion. It is undifferentiated. It falls into the pattern of modern *macro*economics [1] where the attempt is made, perhaps largely under the influence of Keynes, to relate, say, the *total* quantity of money in circulation to *total* employment, *total* output of industry, etc. It is tempting to do so and would simplify economic reasoning enormously if one could discover strict interdependencies. Yet there is great danger in these efforts. For example, the same increase in the quantity of money will have very different consequences when it goes to consumers rather than to producers. This important insight due to the famous though long and still much neglected eighteenth-century economist Cantillon, is obliterated when one restricts oneself to the macroentities.

It is interesting to note that modern science goes in exactly the opposite direction: More and more, finer and finer distinctions are being made. First one has a molecule, then an atom, then the electron, then more and more elementary particles, even subparticles and only by these steps does one arrive at a better understanding of matter. Initially, there was only cancer: Now we know that there may be a hundred different kinds, each with different effects and possibly calling for different treatments. So it is everywhere. But GNP, as an alleged global measure, runs precisely counter to the spirit of modern science even on these grounds.

I am tempted here to quote St. Augustine: "For so it is, oh my Lord God, I measure it, but what it is that I measure I do not know." [2] One might add to St. Augustine: And when it comes to GNP—I even measure it without any error whatsoever!

MEASUREMENT OF WELFARE

When we now talk about "welfare" we are entering upon a field where other, even greater difficulties arise. Economists have struggled with the problem of welfare for centuries. Countless volumes have been written about it, but its measurement has not yet been resolved. It is, therefore, likely that using a primitive notion such as GNP to measure that much disputed concept will come to nought. But first let us examine briefly where the difficulties lie with respect to economic "welfare." Most of us will think at first of our own personal situation: possessions, income, stability of income, needs (as perceived), health, obligations to others, prices of the goods and services to be bought over some more-or-less specified period of time. In short, our personal welfare is composed of many variables. Over time some variables may go up while others go down. Do these movements cancel out? In some cases it is obvious; income may rise in the same proportion as the prices of the goods I want and so all stays the same. But when some prices of relevance to us go up and others go down, then it is not so obvious whether and how individual welfare has been affected.

Men are different in age, incomes, wants, positions, desires. The difficulties arising here would be overcome by broad classifications of people, by the law of large numbers and other such devices. But that still does not tell us about "welfare" because the principal attribute of the latter in the last analysis is what value or utility people attach to their possessions and income. What determines value has puzzled economists for ages. Is there an objective value applicable for everyone, in any circumstance, at any time? How is value produced? What affects value? The answers have ranged from the assertion that there are absolute values to the statement that the economic value of an object is only what you can sell it for: "*Res tantum valet quantum vendi potest,*" which is certainly true for shares on the stock market, though there is also the assertion of an "intrinsic" value which is supposed often to differ in both directions from the sales value.

Although all this may seem to be a confusing situation, there is today no doubt that—apart from the few remaining adherents of the superseded labor-value theory—utility attributed by individuals to goods and services is all that matters. Utility is based on individual preferences and these are related to the objective, technical characteristics of the desired goods and services. The individual can compare the utilities he expects to derive from them even though the goods are all different. Individuals may even be able to construct numbers for their preferences so that they will be better guided in their attempt to obtain a maximum of expected utility by suitable choice and corresponding expenditure over time of their money or other income. This utility, derived from all goods and services, then, is individual, personal welfare.

But here we come to an end: Utility is strictly an individual matter. Exactly the same bundle of goods will have a very different utility for different persons. So much is obvious in a gross sense and need here not be elaborated any further. But what does *not* follow is that we can compare utilities of different individuals. The fact is precisely that different individuals *are* different. Only if they were identical, like the famous Siamese twins, would they have the same utility functions. Perhaps even with them there may be differences because who can look into their brains to make sure that there are no differences in their wishes, preferences, ideas, and ideals? Of course, it is likely that persons in a given income class have similar needs and are concerned about the prices of similar bunches of goods. But if I take a good from A, for whom it has some utility, and give it to B, for whom also it has some utility, it does *not* follow that I have diminished A as much as I have improved B's position. Once more: utilities of different individuals are not comparable. There is now no known way to make them comparable, to find out objectively whether I transfer the same utility (for example, by taxation) from one to the other.

Economists have thought of one way which seems to give us infor- and what GNP is somehow expected to measure. It is the so-called *Pareto optimum,*[3] which says the following: If we look at a community and add a good to one party without at the same time diminishing any other party of that community, then we can say that the welfare of the whole group has increased. This seems plausible and harmless, and we find the Pareto optimum extolled and used in almost every textbook in economics. Yet how can we find out whether this principle holds? Only by questioning—since there is no objective way of making this statement. When does a person feel diminished? This might even happen when something is given to him that he does not want or cannot use (while for others it might be desirable and useful). Does A feel diminished when someone else gets an addition? This can certainly happen even when nothing is actually *taken* from him. It is an entirely different matter whether in a group one individual is given one dollar or one million dollars, though formally the idea of the Pareto optimum is preserved. Common sense tells us otherwise. And how do we even find out whether someone benefits or is diminished? Certainly by interpersonal comparison of utilities, which we know we cannot make. So we have to ask them. Do they tell us the truth? Necessarily? Always? May they not be playing a game in order to extract some greater benefit? So we see that this seemingly innocent and seemingly workable concept is applicable at best under severely restrictive conditions which may never be given in reality.

In reality, we determine, of course, social preferences and act accordingly. We tax people and transfer income to others. We build public works, establish museums, run a military force, and so on. But all this is the product of *political* decision processes, based on voting or on dictates, with only vague ideas of what might be good for the society and increase its "welfare." But there is no strictly scientific unchallengeable basis. There is power or at best persuasion.

The upshot of all this is that "welfare" is an elusive concept—that has, however, great intuitive appeal—but means different things to different people and groups of people. It is a concept that slips through our net the moment we want to make it objective in a scientific sense. I say this with all due respect to the many economists past and present who have given so much thought to this matter. Many valuable attempts have been made, but as so often in science, much has to be discarded that was once considered to be acceptable. There is a great challenge here to economic science to find some day a satisfactory expression and to tell us then also how to measure welfare.

SOCIAL INDICATORS

A promising development is the study of the so-called social indicators. This movement recognizes that a positively valued social development depends on the simultaneous changes in many variables: an increase in production is not unqualifiedly good if it is accompanied by more pollution, or a rise in income without at least no deterioration of its present distribution. Incidentally, note that when I speak of "deterioration of income distribution" I appear to be able to say in a scientifically objective way when a particular income distribution is "better" than another. This would again involve interpersonal comparisons of utility which we know have to be ruled out. Yet common sense tells us that, to take an extreme case, if 90 percent of the national income goes to 5 percent of the population, that country is hardly better off than when possibly even a smaller income is distributed more equally among the inhabitants. This clash of insight with our inability to make scientifically acceptable statements is most disturbing.

There are countless interrelated factors on which welfare, whether personal or communal, depends. Even to describe them, to enumerate them, and to put them into a coherent picture is a difficult task. Any differentiation which leads away from simple global expression is in the right scientific spirit which forces us to make more and more distinctions. There is no doubt that such qualitative, descriptive work has to precede any measurement, and it may give us even now the basis for rough comparisons of different states of the same country and some glimpses of comparing the welfare in different societies.

This is what GNP is supposed to disclose to us—nay, more: even to measure with extraordinary precision! A poorly defined and hard to capture, yet exceedingly important phenomenon such as welfare allegedly measured by another one, GNP, that records nothing better than the total—I am almost inclined to say hodgepodge—of transactions in the economy. The idea has no chance of finding any scientifically valid justification whatsoever. It is once more, as in the case of growth, that one demands of a single, simple, scalar number to produce wonders of measurement.

Of course, attempts have been made to improve upon the GNP concept, for example by considering GDP (gross domestic product) in order to exclude foreign transactions, or attempts to arrive at some measure of *net* output so that the "productivity of an economy" can be determined. Such efforts clearly go in the right direction, namely that one must make finer and finer distinctions. However, conceptual difficulties arise then, too. For example, the notion of "productivity" applies more easily to physical processes where we observe physical inputs and outputs. These can also be expressed in monetary terms though this is not a simple matter. However, in the U.S. economy today perhaps only 40 percent of activity involves physical output; the rest is "services." And no one has come forth with good ideas as to how to measure "productivity" of lawyers, doctors, teachers, policemen, hospitals, scientists, musicians, actors, etc. Yet they all have some kind of "output," conceivably even a "net output." But what is it and how do we compare these heterogeneous services with each other? And though it would be good to differentiate what is hoped for again is a primitive, single, scalar number!

PROBLEMS IN MEASURING GNP

Now let us turn to the way in which one deals with the numbers purporting to measure GNP. Let us forget for the time being all that was said in criticism of GNP. Let us merely look at the measurement itself.

Measurement is demanding, and accurate measurement exceedingly so. It may interest you that even today we do not know the moon's *precise* distance from the earth—though man has visited the moon! What is more, incidentally—and I shall come back to that in an application to economics—we cannot prove, in general, the stability in the large of the moon's orbit around the earth. We can only prove it "in the small." For the whole proof, we would need to know the moon's behavior from the beginning to the end. Exactly the same is true regarding the *entire* planetary system. Should not these two considerations make us economists exceedingly modest and cautious when it comes to the discussion of measurement of complex economic-social situations and to assertions about the stability of the economic universe?

But what happens in reality? Look at the mountains of economic statistics pouring forth continuously from the government and from business: millions of numbers, immense detail, as well as comprehensive aggregates and sophisticated index numbers. Many numbers have been, so to speak, laundered; for example, seasonal variations are eliminated in order to show the alleged true movement of some activities. Some numbers are obtained by carefully studied sampling processes; powerful statistical theory is used in many instances, and sampling errors are carefully spelled out.

But there is one characteristic that pervades all: We virtually never encounter the words "perhaps," "approximately," "about," "maybe," and so on, or see a sign saying: " $\pm$ $\times$ percent." Thus, there is a great difference from the natural sciences where it is customary, nay standard, to ask immediately what the error of observation might be. A notable exception is Simon Kuznets who, in his valuable work on national income,[4] has shown that those figures may have an error in certain classes of income of even more than 20 percent. Though his studies have been gratefully accepted by the economic profession, there is little evidence that those errors are duly considered and that their implication is carried over to other fields. Obviously, if there are errors in aggregates, there are errors in their component parts.

Error there must be. There is no perfect measurement, no matter how good the underlying concept, no matter how fine the measurement tool. Some things seem easy to measure, for example, to count the number of inhabitants in a country; but it may surprise you that in the U.S. Census of 1950,[5] about five million people—equivalent to a good-sized American city, say Chicago—were not counted as was later found out in a careful study.

Other censuses may have been better or worse. In some Asiatic countries the population count is said to have errors of ± 20 percent, and who knows the population of China or of some African countries? For very gross comparisons this may not matter too much, but the frequently and freely used international per capita income data are usually meaningless unless countries are very similar to each other and the time intervals are short.

Errors vary enormously. In physics the finest measurement, I am told, is that of the Ritchie constant, whose error is an unbelievable 10^{-14}. Yet cross-section data for nuclear reactors may have an error of ± 50 percent. But the reactors work! So this shows that the extent of admissible error depends on the use for which the measurement is needed. Of course, the smaller the error, the better. Reduction of error is usually expensive, and how much one wants to spend on error reduction depends again on the importance of the use of the measurement or observation. If a good number has to be combined with a poor one, there is not much point in making the good number even better.

Since errors range from very small to very large, is there a generally accepted standard? The answer is that one should always state honestly what error is involved, in whatever field. This is common in physics, but I regret to say almost totally lacking in economics and the other social sciences. Here I refer to the basic errors in variables, i.e., errors in the basic observations, not to sampling errors and the like. There will have to be a change in attitudes, in demands, in standards. No compromise is possible. It is difficult to determine the various errors because, when the data were put down, no effort was made to discover the inevitable error. And virtually all these numbers are not the result of scientific approaches to the different phenomena. They originate from business transacations, from administrative regulations, etc. Prices are found in shops and factories, export and import quantities; and values are recorded on papers accompanying the commodities; investment figures and profits and total sales are found on financial statements; incomes on income tax returns, and so on.

To give but a few indications of what one finds: Import and export figures of many countries, taken from the respective two sources, often differ by 20, 30 or even 100 percent, both for value and for quantity. This applies even to the trade in gold! The total quantity of money in circulation in the United States is supposedly not known to within perhaps \$20 billion. Yet, pick up almost any basic economic or population statistic and you will find that figures are given without further comment or warning to nine, ten, and more digits. At what point do these figures lose their significance? Is it the same point in all series, in a majority of series? No discussion, no commentary, nothing: just an uncritical abandonment to figures.

GNP AS MEASURE OF GROWTH

Now we come to the point of looking at the calculations which are made with the GNP figures.

It is well to start by quoting a statement made by one of the greatest mathematicians of all time, C. F. W. Gauss: "The lack of mathematical insight shows up in nothing as surprisingly as in unbounded precision in numerical computations." There are countless illustrations for such activity, not only in economics, but in all social sciences. This is another sign for their lack of maturity compared to the physical sciences. There seems to be a love for meaningless digits. Norbert Wiener, also an eminent mathematician, upon looking at material described in my book, *On the Accuracy of Economic Observations,* published by Princeton University Press in 1963, observed to me: "Economics is a one-digit science." I would be inclined to say that that is true for parts of it, but there are a few parts where two, perhaps even three, digits are admissible, and where our power of interpretation is great enough to handle such fine detail.

The principal calculations to which GNP figures are subjected are rates of change, presumably rates of *growth,* because that is with what the world has been made aware. Governments everywhere look hypnotized at these calculations and are judged by the number generated even for the short intervals of a quarter year—incidentally, so brief a period that one must be astonished that (even given modern means of communications) all the hundreds of thousands of underlying figures could be collected—all this without any error whatsoever! Or, if —heaven forbid—there are errors that they very kindly distribute themselves in such manner that they all cancel out?

The facts are, of course, quite the contrary. There must be errors; after all, we live in a "stochastic universe," which means that the world is to a large measure indeterminate. And that errors in economic observations would cancel out precisely—of that no one has given proof and no one will ever be able to do so in general.

I shall give two illustrations of calculations. Suppose you have two consecutive GNP numbers—whatever their absolute values be—such that the second one is 3 percent larger than the first one, assuming each one to be perfect. Now assume there was a 1 percent error in each figure. Thus, if the first year should have been 1 percent lower and the second year 1 percent higher, then the rate of growth, instead of being 3 percent, is in fact +5.08 percent. Quite a difference! But if, the other way around, the first year should have been 1 percent higher than reported and the second year should have been 1 percent lower, then the rate of growth is only 0.96 percent instead of 3 percent. What is "reality"? A *one* percent error, one way or the other, is tiny by almost all standards. Recall that in physics, a paradigm for measurement, an observation with only a 3 percent error is frequently a very good and useful measurement. What happens to our growth rates if we repeat what was just done for 1 percent now for ±3 percent? In the first case, instead of the error-free 3 percent basic change, we obtain a growth rate of +9.37 percent; in the second case, a decline of growth by 3 percent. So the economy, as represented by an alleged error-free change in GNP statistics, instead of having grown by 3 percent, could actually have grown by 9.37 percent or decreased by 3 percent. This is the result of trivial calculations. Precisely for being so trivial these figures show the grossness of the (tacit) assertion that the "true" rate of change, or "growth," is allegedly 3 percent.

Of course, if the errors in the two underlying GNP figures would go in the same direction—i.e., being each either positive or negative—and in addition were to be *identical*, then nothing would change; the rate would stay the same. But even if they should go in the same direction but were to differ from each other in consecutive years, the rate of change would no longer remain at the alleged error-free value.

Simple as these considerations are, they are basic. They illustrate precisely the importance of the quoted statement from Gauss. To make matters worse, one is now no longer satisfied with yearly comparisons, but uses quarterly data. For these, the same arguments apply. In fact, the situation is worse, because in gathering the thousands of underlying figures, there are delays, corrections, etc., in spite of the availability of electronic computers at certain stages. This is true whether yearly or quarterly figures are collected. The respective statistical offices naturally want to do as good a job as possible and so they are led to *correct* the initially given figures because errors are discovered over time. Indeed, the yearly GNP, or even the much finer National Income Statistics, often take up to *ten* years until the final figure is presented. In the course of these successive revisions there are plus and minus changes. Expressed as percentages of the intially given figures the revisions are of the order of 2, 3, or sometimes more percent. And over the years, some corrections go up, some go down for the *same* year. Clearly, quarterly figures are subject to even more, and also bigger corrections. Now all this plays havoc with the initially calculated rate of change, presumably of growth. Finally, even when after many years a definite figure is stated (different always from the first one!), that figure is not and can not be free of some remaining error of observations. Recall that no measurement is absolute, that we live in a stochastic universe, and that science—no matter how well developed—is only an approximation to reality.

Now it is peculiar that governments are voluntarily submitting to be judged by primitive numbers such as those here discussed. It is not that one would want to deny that there exists some intuitive notion of "growth," that some part of this phenomenon can be expressed numerically. But the objection is that all can be put into one single number that is free of all possible faults. That is unacceptable. What is more, these numbers are supposed to be comparable over long periods of time and internationally. Whether it be India or Sweden or China or Japan or the United States, the precise rates of growth are compared with each other. For some countries even the number of inhabitants is only vaguely known. It is difficult to see why statesmen would expose themselves to this kind of evaluation.

Economists have to share in the blame. They have introduced the notion of "fine tuning" of the economy, the idea that one could control the whole economy so precisely that its performance could be judged by the second or even third digits of growth rates, when in truth even the first digit is in doubt. One hears a little less, however, about the fine tuning recently in view of the fact that rather gross events such as much unemployment, high interest rates, steep monopolistically controlled oil price increases are with us. "Fine tuning" would require frequent switches in policy given the many factors which determine economic life. But such switches are not only not welcome but can hardly be made, given the inherent slowness in political processes and the slowness with which they become effective.

CONCLUSION

We would, of course, like to know whether and how much and in what direction the economy has grown and how economic welfare has been changed, presumably been improved. We would like to have good, trustworthy numerical expressions for both. Alas, the GNP concept is primitive in the extreme and certainly of little value for any adequate expression of "growth." "Social welfare" is still so difficult and controversial a notion that, without overcoming the inherent great conceptual difficulties, we cannot indicate any measure at present which is scientifically unchallengeable and does not involve political, moral, or whatever other prejudices.

NOTES

1. There are several dozen textbooks on macroeconomics. Cf., e.g., P. Wonnacott's of that title (Homewood, Ill.: Irwin, 1974).
2. This is quoted by W. Allen Wallis from *The Confession of St. Augustine,* in *Goal of Economic Growth,* edited by E. S. Phelps (New York: W. W. Norton, 1962), which in turn is quoted in A. Rubner, *Three Sacred Cows of Economics* (New York: Barnes and Noble, 1971), p. 23. This very readable and competent book is highly recommended for its critical examination of great masses of interesting material pertaining to growth, forecasting, and planning.
3. Cf. O. Morgenstern, "Pareto Optimum and Economic Organization," in *Systeme und Methoden in den Wirtschafts- und Sozia-wissenschaften* (Tübingen: N. Kloten a.o. Eds., J. C. B. Mohr, 1964), pp. 573–586; and O. Morgenstern, "Thirteen Critical Points in Contemporary Economic Theory," *Journal of Economic Literature,* Vol. 10, No. 4 (1972), pp. 1163–1189.

4. Simon N. Kuznets, *National Income and Its Composition* (New York: National Bureau of Economic Research, 1942).

5. A. J. Coale and M. Zelnick, *New Estimates of Fertility and Population in the U.S.; a Study of Annual White Births from 1855 to 1960 and of Completeness of Enumeration in the Censuses from 1880 to 1960* (Princeton, N.J.: Princeton University Press, 1963).

FIVE

Social Indicators and Corporate Social Performance: A Case of Delayed Parallelism

Eleanor Bernert Sheldon

President, Social Science Research Council

and

Robert Parke

*Director, Center For Coordination of Research on
Social Indicators,
Social Science Research Council*

What is the relationship between social indicators and corporate social performance? In order to better comprehend what we have to say about that relationship, we must examine: (1) What are social indicators? (2) What is involved in measuring corporate social performance? (3) How, if at all, do the two intersect?

To establish realistic expectations, it is instructive to review the development of interest in social indicators, to discuss the various uses that have been claimed for them, and to see what the actual results of this interest have been.

SOCIAL INDICATORS

By social indicators we mean statistical time series that measure changes in significant aspects of a society. That society may be as small as a neighborhood or as comprehensive as the society of nations; moreover, not all observers will agree on what features of the society are significant for indicator purposes. Nonetheless, a social indicator constitutes a measure of the structure, functioning, or condition of that society, which permits quantitative comparison over time. Researchers in the field are doing conceptual, methodological, and data development work in order to provide measures of change in such varied areas as social mobility, subjective sense of well-being, tolerance of dissent, and many others, and to develop analytical models which account for such changes.

Many examples of social indicators may be found in a recent publication by that title, compiled in the U.S. Office of Management and Budget. *Social Indicators, 1973* consists of charts and tables presenting statistical time series for the United States, selected and organized around eight "social concerns," namely, health, public safety, education, employment, income, housing, leisure and recreation, and population.[1] That report, which represents an important first step by the U.S. government, has been the subject of much professional comment, including criticism on both conceptual and statistical grounds.[2] We draw on some of that discussion here because, by describing how the report was designed and suggesting how it might be done differently, we hope to convey something of the character of current work on social indicators and to suggest directions that further work should pursue. For *Social Indicators, 1973* reflects not only the rather primitive state of development of social indicators; it also reflects a particular set of choices with reference to live issues in the field.

First, as the list of topics in *Social Indicators, 1973* suggests, the effort is to present *noneconomic* measures of well-being. Even in the income chapter, the report devotes more attention to poverty and changes in the distribution of income than it does to changes in aggregate per capita income. While this emphasis is consistent with much of the literature on social indicators, there is a danger that efforts to transcend economic indicators end up by ignoring them. By contrast, some research on social indicators has taken economic data as the point of departure, tracing the ramification of economic changes into other fields. An official social report for Japan, for example, has used data on elasticity of demand for goods and services to show how rising affluence has altered the Japanese standard of living.[3]

We have several short series of survey data on the responses of Americans to the fuel shortage in the winter of 1973–74. These include information on whom people blamed for the shortages, whether people felt they were getting their fair share of fuel, and how they modified their fuel consuming behavior.[4] In addition, work is under way to develop measures of changes in people's sense of the fairness of their pay, measures which should be most illuminating in a time of high unemployment and rapid inflation.[5] In a society dominated by institutions of production and marketing, monitoring the social consequences of the operation of those institutions ought to be a major item on the agenda for social indicators.

Second, in its text and its selection of data, *Social Indicators, 1973* emphasizes measures of *individual* rather than institutional or societal well-being. The aim is to present measures of the distribution of goods and bads among individuals in the society rather than measures reflecting the changing state of the body politic as reflected in declining popular trust in government, changes in the fluidity of the society as reflected by changes in social mobility, or the changing fortunes of voluntary associations such as the church. Some degree of individualistic emphasis such as that in *Social Indicators, 1973* is surely appropriate in an individualistic nation. But measures of the changing fortunes of individuals cannot substitute for measures of the changing state of society. Measures of the functioning of the collectivity have a key contribution to make both to understanding and to social policy based on it.

Third, the report seeks to focus on the *outputs* of social systems rather than the *inputs* to them; that is to say, it emphasizes measures of social conditions, including those which government activities are supposed to affect such as the knowledge and health of the population, rather than measures of budget size or program activity in educational or health care institutions. For example, the chapter on crime includes survey data on the number of people victimized by crime, not just the conventional statistics on the crimes reported to the police, which are to a large degree measures of the activities of police rather than of the incidence of crime.

The distinction between the inputs and outputs of government programs has been a useful one. It has reminded us not to accept statistics on school budgets as substitutes for measures of what schooling is accomplishing. Unfortunately, the distinction has become reified, and we have tended to forget that what is input for one part of the system is output for another. Thus, teacher/pupil ratios are discarded as irrelevant as measures of pupil learning, and the fact that such figures may tell us something important about the working conditions of teachers is overlooked.

More important, the exclusive emphasis on the measurement of outputs as the function of social indcators results in too little attention being given to factors which cause the output measures to change. If we recognize the interconnectedness of society and if we hope to understand the processes by which change occurs, we must be ready to incorporate in our analysis much that does not satisfy the narrow criterion of "outputs" expressed as "individual welfare." Indeed, lacking a suitable explanatory framework, it is hazardous to interpret changes in observations as measures of changes in welfare.

Fourth, within the rather severe limits of available data, *Social Indicators, 1973* emphasizes the *subjective aspects* of well-being, such as job satisfaction (as distinguished from more objective measures such as employment) and survey data on the number of people who say they are afraid to walk out at night (which is for many purposes a more important statistic than the number of crimes reported to the police). The recognition which *Social Indicators, 1973* accords to work on subjective indicators is welcome, even though the relations between subjective measures and objective measures are poorly understood and there are many anomalous relationships (e.g., studies in several cities have reported that fear of crime is highest in the suburbs, whereas reported criminal acts are highest in the inner city).

Social Indicators, 1973 is the U.S. contribution to a large and growing body of national reports on social trends. As such, it is a fairly typical recent product of the social indicators movement.

THE SOCIAL INDICATORS MOVEMENT

"Social Indicators," and allied phrases—"social accounting," "social reporting," and "monitoring social change"—came into use by social scientists, commentators, and policy makers in the mid-1960s. These phrases and the ideas they represented emerged from an awareness of rapid social change; from a sense of emerging and extant problems with origins deep in the social structure; from the ambience of the early Johnson administration which encompassed a commitment to the idea that the benefits and costs of domestic social programs are subject to measurement; and from the belief that each newly perceived, albeit ancient, inadequacy in the society should, and would, call forth a corrective response from a federal government whose efficacy would be assisted by social measurement, planning, and new management analytical techniques.

Impetus was provided by a handful of social scientists and public administrators. The enthusiasm elicited responses from economists who saw a role for their skills as theorists and measurers of welfare; sociologists who saw the relevance of their own research tradition in the measurement of social trends; political scientists who sought ways to rationalize government programs; social workers, public administrators, and a broad array of other social researchers and practitioners. Out of their work emerged what came to be known as the "social indicators movement," an apt designation in that, as in all movements in their initial stages, the participants were ill-defined as to membership; they had little organization, and scarcely a few shared specific objectives; they did share some celebrated but necessarily ambiguous symbols; and they were led by able and articulate visionaries.

Use of the phrase "social indicators" became widespread following publication of a book by that title in 1966.[6] This and other early documents asserted a need to develop and utilize time-series statistics to measure the social state of the nation with respect to a broad range of consensus values, or sometimes more narrowly national goals. Associated with this were expressions of need for measures of noneconomic dimensions of well-being approaching the power of available economic statistics.[7] Underlying these expressions was a commitment to the idea that better social information would improve public policy.

These ideas received an influential statement in *Toward a Social Report,* issued by the Department of Health, Education, and Welfare in 1969.[8] Avowedly not a social report, but a step in that direction, the volume was presented as "an attempt on the part of social scientists, to look at several important areas and digest what is known about progress toward generally accepted goals." The areas treated were health; social mobility; the condition of the physical environment; income and property; public order and safety; and learning, science, and art.

The demands for social information relevant to public policy decisions were couched in terms of the limitations of purely economic considerations in dealing with social problems of modern American society. Policies and programs aimed at alleviation of problems seek data for planning, for implementation—and eventually for evaluation. Objectives for these demands for social information were stated in the following terms: social information (indicators) is required for (1) use in the establishment of social goals and priorities; (2) the evaluation of public programs; and (3) for the development of a system of social accounts that could provide guidance among alternative interventions.[9]

These are big claims, and two of them—the alleged role of indicators in setting priorities and in evaluating programs—are particularly relevant for this discussion *and* are demonstrably fallacious, as we shall see. The ambition underlying both claims—the ambition to use statistics to rationalize management and policy making—is embedded in both and thus merits our attention.

SETTING GOALS AND PRIORITIES

It would be foolish to argue against the use of indicators in program planning and development. But it is also naive to hold that social indicators in themselves permit decisions on priority setting. "The use of data to make a case either already decided on other grounds or one that inevitably is going to be determined by political rather than 'objective' considerations—whether or not it is in a good cause—is a weak basis for the indicator effort. Priorities do not depend on assembled data. Rather, they stem from national objectives and values and their hierarchical ordering." [10]

Peter J. Henriot has stated: "In short, when used for purposes of setting goals and priorities, indicators must be regarded as inputs into a complex political mosaic. That they are potentially powerful tools in the development of social policy is not to be denied. But they do not make social policy development any more objective. Advocates of policy can strengthen their position by citing hard data and so can critics of these policies." [11] Management and policy making are political and social processes in which information (be it statistical or not) is merely a technical input. Let us provide an example:

Early in 1974, the U.S. Commissioner of Labor Statistics announced the impending issuance of a revised consumer price index. A major survey of consumer purchasing habits was nearing completion, which would provide new weights for the components in the consumer "market basket." The index weights had not been updated for more than a decade, and government statisticians had been preparing carefully for a new index series which would more truly reflect the impact of contemporary price changes on a more representative group of consumers.

The announcement elicited a storm of influential protest. A union president made it clear that the old CPI was quite satisfactory for purposes of his constituents: It was observed that the CPI is incorporated in the escalator clauses of major national labor-management contracts (indeed, we are informed that the CPI is built into one contract that does not expire until 1980). It is a reasonable surmise that the opponents of change felt that revisions in the bases of the index would, in effect, alter the terms of a key part of those contracts. As a consequence of the protest, the Bureau of Labor Statistics will publish the CPI on both the old and the new bases, at least for a while.

It is clear that the CPI serves an important social and political function more or less independent of its informational function. It is a mechanism for conflict resolution; by agreeing to escalator clauses keyed to the CPI, labor and management eliminate a large arena for dispute requiring negotiations between them. Ezrahi has written of similar protests over consumer price index revision in World War II:

> . . . any changes designed to update and modify the index in order to make it more scientifically adequate could have destabilized a delicate system of social arrangements. . . . The involved parties obviously looked at the index as a regulatory or coordinating tool which is not sustained on grounds of scientific validity, but rather as a convenient convention which would endure as long as the balance of benefits to the interested parties outweighed the costs.[12]

EVALUATION OF PROGRAMS

Statistical time-series that provide measures of social change—social indicators—are simply unsuitable for evaluating the impact of programs. In this case, it is not the political naiveté of the claim which attracts our attention, but its technical or logical inappropriateness. It is simply the wrong scientific strategy. Through the development and analysis of descriptive time-series and the modeling of social processes, we will be able to describe the state of the society and its dynamics and thus improve immensely our ability to state problems in a productive fashion, obtain clues as to promising lines of endeavor, and ask good questions. But these activities cannot measure program effectiveness. To do that, we must adopt a strategy that enables us to demonstrate that the program, not uncontrolled extraneous variables, determines the outcomes measured by indicators.

There is, among social scientists, increasing recognition that, from a scientific point of view, the most satisfactory way to demonstrate this is to incorporate experimental designs into the testing of programs.[13] Although references to program evaluation were abundant in the early discussions of social indicators, increasingly there seems to be concurrence with a view which distinguishes the descriptive and analytical statistical time-series needed to monitor and analyze social change from the experimental designs by which programs may be evaluated.

By way of summary: Goal and priority setting are political

processes; indicators are part of the process, but play quite a different role than envisioned in the notion that they serve to rationalize management. As for evaluation, indicators are the wrong scientific strategy; evaluation research, particularly social experimentation, is the right one.

SOCIAL INDICATORS TODAY

What *can* social indicators do? What have been the actual useful results from all the early enthusiasm? The interest in social indicators has stimulated a revival of interest in quantitative, comparative, social analysis,[14] in the analysis of social change, in conceptual and measurement work on such topics as prejudice, crime, and learning, and in the development of models of social processes. The fruit of these efforts will be more directly a contribution to the policy maker's cognition and understanding of his problems than to his actual decision.

This work takes two forms: (1) descriptive measures and their reporting; and (2) analytical studies of social change. It serves two functions: information and enlightenment. It answers two questions: what happened, and why? Let us provide examples of descriptive and analytical studies that serve these functions.

There is a statistical report which casts an entirely new light on the policy discussions of what to do about the alleged deterioration in the quality of working life. Surveys taken from 1958 to 1973 were reanalyzed to determine whether there has been a *trend* in job satisfaction in the United States. From the data presented, the authors conclude, "there has *not* been any significant decrease in overall levels of job satisfaction in the past decade." They also examine "the much-discussed large recent decline in job satisfaction of younger workers," and find no such decline, concluding: "Younger workers have been consistently less satisfied than their elders for the last 15 years and probably even earlier than that." [15]

The inference from these findings is not that we should be unconcerned with something called "the quality of working life" but that, if we are to worry about it and mount programs to change it, we should do so for the right reasons and with a sense of urgency informed by the facts. Reasons for acting do not include a perceptible decline in job satisfaction in recent years, for none can be perceived.

The work of Duncan and Blau, and subsequently of Hauser and Featherman, on the measurement of occupational mobility in the United States, has provided high-quality measures of changes in social mobility and measures of the role played by family background, race, and education in the mobility process.[16] These scholars measure mobility, not the effects of Headstart or the Job Corps program. The focus is on what happened to the conditions that policies and programs are presumed to affect, not the far more difficult question of what effect those programs had on those conditions. Their work provides enlightenment—understanding of how the society works; it provides a frame of reference for thinking about programs, but makes no direct contribution to setting goals and priorities. These are valuable, though perhaps limited, contributions. The recognized contribution of social indicators work, as distinguished from its rhetoric, is aptly stated by Duncan:

> The value of improved measures of social change . . . is not that they necessarily resolve theoretical issues concerning social dynamics or settle pragmatic issues of social polity, but that they may permit those issues to be argued more productively.[17]

CORPORATE SOCIAL RESPONSIBILITY

What is the phenomenon we are dealing with when we refer to corporate social responsibility? First of all, we should be reminded that the very concept of socially responsible business has existed since the time of the ancient Greeks, who were offended by the notion that wealth was to be used as its owner wishes without attending to the "interests of humanity and of social consequences." Medieval-period merchants couched their business ethics in the language of the church—the justification for business rests in the merchants' intentions; if his prime objective was profit, then he was sinfully engaged; his proper duty was to earn a livelihood and to help the good of his neighbor. Money was a means to an end, and trade was to be performed honestly and well.[18]

More recently, and again as an outgrowth of conditions similar to those contributing to the rise of the social-indicators movement both here and abroad, social responsiveness is being demanded of our institutions, including business. Among those who focus on business institutions, we find wide variation in their demands; we find scarcely any shared specific objectives; the participants are ill-defined and have little organization; they do share some celebrated but ambiguous symbols; and they are led by some able and articulate visionaries —characteristics of the earlier social indicator movement.

Before proceeding to delineate the parallelisms further, we would like to describe three major approaches characterizing the relationship of business to society. It is not irrelevant to our later comments on the measurement of corporate social performance.

The first is that of "traditional" business and stems from the early industrial era. Business operates in a competitive market and functions to make profit; hence, the businessman is required only to deal fairly and honestly with his clients. The question of how one makes a profit or for what purpose is not particularly germane to the businessman qua businessman. Those who are committed to this attitude and who do make contributions to the general welfare do so primarily by serving in community or charitable organizations.

The second view has been gaining ground since the turn of the century. This approach holds that business has a responsibility to society with respect to its employees and products, and a responsibility to mirror the ideals and values of the society within its own microcosm. Businessmen then act affirmatively to promote safety, honesty, and efficiency; to contain and eliminate where possible those disruptions to the environment caused by their products or processes; and to create within their own institutions the conditions of nondiscrimination demanded by society.

The third viewpoint is an activist one. It is held more by critics of business than by businessmen: It is a primary obligation of business to use its power to promote social ends perceived as moral. An obvious example from the recent past: by refusing to sell to government unless the government withdraws from the Vietnam war or refusing to deal with other corporations whose services may further the prosecution of the war. (Other examples are South Africa or Angola.)

Those holding the traditional view rely on "market mechanisms" or government programs to resolve social issues. Direct action is often considered to be inappropriate—a diversion of management skills or a violation of responsibility to the owners. Those taking the second view find it desirable to address social problems aggressively within the scope of "normal business activities" (manufacturers exercising control of their pollution, minority recruitment and training programs; financial institutions providing loans for pollution control, for the development of black businesses). The activist view seeks the use of corporate influence and action in social areas not usually associated with normal business functioning. Within business, we find a telephone company sponsoring clinics on drug abuse, or a university voting its shares of stock on a political resolution unrelated to the conduct of a company's business.

CORPORATE SOCIAL AUDITS

Concomitant with the wide-ranging demands for socially responsive business institutions, expressed in a voluminous normative literature on business policy, the notion of a "corporate social audit" has emerged. This notion, often coupled with that of "corporate social accounts" and perhaps not differentiated from it, has provided many programmatic statements and proposals for the development of such an instrument. Raymond Bauer and others [19] have written extensively on the subject and have examined its conceptual bases, the problems of measurement, and actual attempts to conduct social audits.

An examination of the literature on corporate social responsibility and the measurement of its performance yields terms reminiscent of the earlier social indicator literature: Business has responsibilities beyond those of strictly economic considerations; as a social institution in a society plagued by problems, it must partake of the activities aimed at the alleviation of these problems. Business must devise policies and programs relevant to the alleviation effort. Therefore, it must have data for planning and implementation purposes—eventually for evaluation. Again, we find that data are required for: (1) management decisions on goals and priorities; and (2) the evaluation of programs. Thus, social audits or accounts or some other tool will assess the social performance of a corporation in as systematic manner as our current audits and accounting procedures assess corporate financial performance.

Not wishing to belabor the obvious fallacies here, let us remind you of our earlier comments about these claims for social indicators: (1) management decision- and policy-making are political and social processes in which data and other information are merely technical inputs. There is nothing inherent in the system that could lead one to conclude that such inputs will necessarily increase the rationality of management. (2) Statistical time-series do not control for extraneous factors that influence program outcomes and thus are inadequate for program evaluation.

THE ROLE OF SOCIAL INDICATORS

The topic "The Role of Social Indicators" is sufficiently vague to allow such comments on the parallelisms between the two efforts. We have focused on the similarities between the developments of the "social indicator movement" and what appears to be a "corporate social audit movement" not only to highlight the striking similarities in the rationales underpinning the two endeavors, but primarily to signalize the weaknesses of their initial intended purposes. Before concluding, then, we would like to examine the more positive and possible relationship.

Bauer has stated: "Conceptually, the corporation may be thought of as a purposive social organization that pursues its objectives in an environmental system with which it must maintain a reasonable equilibrium."[20] That environment, as Bauer has pointed out, can be divided into the "task environment" and the "purpose-giving environment." The former relates to traditional business concerns (the marketplace, technology, capital, labor); and the latter is the sociopolitical system within which business operates—it defines mores and values, and establishes and enforces society's priorities. Traditionally, American business has responded to and initiated change in its task environment and, while at times responsive, it has generally tended to resist change in the sociopolitical system. The purpose-giving environment has been changing rapidly, and its demands on the corporation have increased. More recently, there seems to be a growing tendency for business to take a more responsive and perhaps a more initiating role in this purposive environment.

A responsive corporation might be involved in at least the first three of the following four functions:

1. Detection and definition of issues
2. Selection of issues to which to become committed
3. Implementation of policies involving these issues
4. Accountability to the public.

It is to the first of these functions that the results of research on social indicators might contribute. Currently, that research (in contrast to some of the earlier rhetoric about it) is aimed at providing a descriptive and analytic picture of our society and its changes over time. Work is being mounted on improving the data base for such descriptions and analyses, on examining and refining our concepts and measures, and on providing new ones and models of their relationships. As a result of these developments, we will be increasingly able "to describe the state of society and its dynamics and thus improve immensely our ability to state problems in a productive fashion, obtain clues as to promising lines of endeavor. . . . The issue [therefore] is not whether social indicators are useful for policy but, rather, how this usefulness comes about." [21] Though we cannot provide the formula for priority selection and program evaluation, we can assist in the detection and definition of issues confronting the nation's institutions.

By way of summary, we repeat: The role of social indicators in the development of the measurement of corporate performance is not in their usefulness for priority setting or program evaluation; it rests rather in the promise to provide answers to a few simple questions: What does our society look like? How is it changing, and why? We trust that this is a significant role.

NOTES

1. U.S. Office of Management and Budget, *Social Indicators, 1973* (Washington, D.C.: GPO, 1974).
2. Roxann Van Dusen, ed., *Social Indicators, 1973: A Review Symposium* (New York: Social Science Research Council, 1974).
3. Japan Economic Planning Agency, *Whitepaper on National Life 1973: The Life and Its Quality in Japan* (Tokyo: Overseas Data Service Co., Ltd., 1973).
4. "Continuous National Survey, Results for the Period November 15, 1973 through February 7, 1974" (Chicago: National Opinion Research Center, 1974), mimeograph.
5. Burkhard Strumpel, "Economic Well-Being as an Object of Social Measurement," in *Subjective Elements of Well-Being,* edited by B. Strumpel (Paris: Organization for Economic Cooperation and Development, 1974).
6. Raymond Bauer, ed., *Social Indicators* (Cambridge, Mass.: M.I.T. Press, 1966).
7. U.S. President's Commission on Technology, Automation, and Economic Progress, *Technology and the American Economy* (Washington, D.C.: 1966); Bertram Gross, ed., *The Annals* of the American Academy of Political and Social Sciences (March and September 1967); *Congressional Record Senate,* S15314, "Full Opportunity and National Goals and Priorities" (September 1973).
8. U.S. Department of Health, Education, and Welfare, *Toward a Social Report* (Washington, D.C.: 1969).
9. Eleanor Bernert Sheldon and Kenneth C. Land, "Social Reporting for the 1970's: A Review and Programmatic Statement," *Policy Sciences,* Vol. 3 (1972), pp. 137–151.
10. Eleanor Bernert Sheldon and Howard Freeman, "Notes on Social Indicators: Promises and Potential," *Policy Sciences,* Vol. 1 (1970), pp. 99–100.
11. Peter J. Henriot, "Political Questions about Social Indicators," *Western Political Quarterly,* Vol. 23 (June 1970).
12. Yaron Ezrahi, "Indicators and the Political State of Science," first draft,

p. 28. Prepared for the Conference on Science Indicators (Stanford, Calif.: Center for Advanced Study in the Behavioral Sciences, June 1974).

13. Alice M. Rivlin, *Systematic Thinking for Social Action* (Washington, D.C.: The Brookings Institution, 1971); "Social Experiments: Their Uses and Limitations," *Monthly Labor Review*, (June 1974), pp. 28–35; Henry W. Riecken and Robert F. Boruch *et al.*, eds., *Experimentation as a Method for Planning and Evaluating Social Intervention* (New York: Academic Press, 1974); Donald Campbell, "Reforms as Experiments," *American Psychologist* (1969), pp. 409–429.

14. Eleanor Bernert Sheldon and Robert Parke, "Social Indicators," *Science*, May 16, 1975, pp. 693–99.

15. R.P. Quinn, G. L. Stanes, and M. R. McCullough, *Job Satisfaction: Is There a Trend?*, Manpower Research Monograph No. 30 (Washington, D.C.: U.S. Department of Labor, Manpower Administration, 1974).

16. David L. Featherman and Robert M. Hauser, "Design for a Replicated Study of Social Mobility in the United States," in *Social Indicator Models*, edited by Kenneth Land and Seymour Spilerman (New York: Russell Sage Foundation, 1975); Peter M. Blau and Otis Dudley Duncan, *The American Occupational Structure* (New York: Wiley, 1967).

17. Otis Dudley Duncan, "Measuring Social Change Via Replication of Surveys," in Land and Spilerman, *op. cit.*

18. Eleanor Bernert Sheldon, "Foreword," in Raymond A. Bauer and Dan H. Fenn, Jr., *The Corporate Social Audit* (New York: Russell Sage Foundation, 1972), pp. iii–vi.

19. Bauer and Fenn, *op. cit.;* Meinolf Dierkes and Raymond A. Bauer, eds., *Corporate Social Accounting* (New York: Praeger, 1973); Raymond A. Bauer *et al.*, "The Development of Corporate Responsiveness: Empirical Research on the Changing Role of Business, A Progress Report" (unpublished, 1974).

20. Raymond A. Bauer, "The Future of Corporate Social Accounting," in Dierkes and Bauer, *op. cit.*, p. 389.

21. Sheldon and Parke, *op. cit.*

SIX

The Corporate Social Audit

David F. Linowes

Partner, Laventhol Krekstein Horwath & Horwath
Worldwide Auditors and Consultants

INTRODUCTION

In recent times the corporation has become an integral part of the functioning of our nation. In addition to being the beneficiary of the privileges and rights which it has been granted by the state, it is now being required to assume responsibility toward the society in which it operates.

Some would argue that a corporation's responsibility to society is as old as the corporation itself. Centuries ago, corporate charters were awarded only by special acts of the king or Parliament, and only to do something government wanted done. During the last century in this country railroad corporations were chartered to create access to the West so that our nation's resources could be more effectively exploited and so that the frontier of our nation could be opened up for settlement, all of which our government was anxious to bring about.

Over the years, the nature of authorization to create a corporation began to change and corporate charters have been granted by states merely for the asking, and by the payment of quite nominal fees. This has evolved only in the past century.

In previous decades, it had always been assumed that the vast expanses of water, land, and air could absorb the wastes of production and neutralize any potential harmful elements. Man assumed the natural environment would always renew itself. We now know this is not so.

We are a society in transition. Traditional concepts are being challenged and in the process some fiefdoms are toppling. Although a socioeconomic revolution is in force, in my judgment, one thing seems certain. The organizations that will survive and flourish are not those that bitterly oppose the transition or seek to block the restructuring, but those organizations that adjust to rational change and help pioneer it. Inevitably, we must move to ever more cooperation between the private sector and the public sector. Economic goals of corporate business can no longer be separated from the social goals of government.

Business corporations themselves have been changing and at the same time have become so massive that they exercise important influences on the communities in which they operate. Often they strongly influence the laws to which they are required to conform. As a matter of fact, the entire private sector has become all mixed up with the public sector.

It can be argued that we are witnessing what might be considered a strict constructionist approach to the nature and authority of the corporate concept. This return to corporate license basics appears to have been triggered largely because we have suddenly awakened to the phenomenon that our present-day, comfort-centered society is being threatened by pollution of land, sea, and air. And, to an increasing degree, corporations have been creating the conditions that have resulted in many social ills, not by choice or design. But, inherent in our massive, complex, rapidly mushrooming free enterprise system is the inevitability of social abuses, some germane to the profit pursuit, some thoughtless, a small minority negligent or unscrupulous. Everyone agrees that to permit these conditions to continue must inevitably lead to social suicide. Steps must be taken to correct the abuses.

ATTITUDES OF BUSINESS

Is this apparent evolution in corporate business administration being recognized by those industrial leaders directly concerned? What are business executives saying about all of this?

The Council of Trends and Perspective of the Chamber of Commerce of the U.S. made a study of corporate social responsibility [1] and concluded with eight findings and recommendations. Here are three of them:

Finding: The social responsibility of business movement is progressing from an initial stage in which many business firms are recognizing their new responsibilities to the planning and action stages.

Recommendation: Business corporations should design a social policy, meaning that they must include in their accounting the indirect costs to society of their operation to the extent possible; integrate social considerations into their decisions and implement other social policies.

Finding: Many business social goals are capable of being set, evaluated and monitored in the same way as are traditional business goals.

Recommendation: Wherever possible, in evaluating and monitoring its social performance, each business firm should quantify costs and benefits in order to help plan and measure its social action programs, to help communicate its social policy both within the firm and with outside groups and to justify the economic feasibility of the programs.

Finding: Although social auditing is a new concept, many business firms are preparing audits of certain aspects of their social performance as a result of inspections and hearings conducted by such Federal agencies as the Equal Employment Opportunity Commission, the Occupational Safety and

Health Administration, and the Environmental Protection
Agency.

Recommendation: To provide another view of how its social policy is
being implemented, each involved business firm should
develop a social auditing procedure. Such an audit should at
first be conducted by its own personnel, if qualified personnel
are available. Subsequently, outside professional auditors
might be engaged to conduct the social audit.

Obviously, representatives of corporate business in America are
recognizing the enlarged mandate with which business is being
charged by society, and is urging wholesome responsiveness.

In an attempt to determine the current business practices in assess-
ing the social activities of corporations, the Committee for Economic
Development conducted a survey of 880 companies during the past
year.[2] Replies were received from 284 companies. One of the questions
asked was whether the company had inventoried or assessed what it
had done in certain specific social fields. Seventy-six percent reported
that they had made such an inventory or assessment since January 1,
1972. That is, about three-fourths of the companies had performed a
form of "social audit."

In response to the question, "Has your company given any person,
organizational unit or group responsibility for surveying more or less
continuously the evolving demands on your company for social action
programs?" 70 percent answered that they had assigned such
responsibility.

Questions also were designed to determine why companies undertook social audits. Seven out of ten indicated they did so either to
identify those social programs which the management thought it
ought to be pursuing; to examine what the company was doing in
selected areas; to evaluate its performance in the social areas selected;
to inject into the general thinking of managers a social point of view; to
assure that decision-making processes incorporate social points of view;
or to inform the public of what the company is doing. That is, 70
percent of the companies performed such audits voluntarily, for their
own management purposes.

One-fourth of the companies indicated they took the social evaluations either to determine areas where the company might be vulnera-

ble to attack; to meet public demand for accountability; to identify those social programs the company felt pressured to undertake; or to offset irresponsible audits made by outside groups. That is, only 25 percent of the companies undertook social audits because of some kind of outside pressure, real or imagined.

It is of interest to note that 39 percent of the companies made their social audit reports available to the general public, whereas 38 percent routed them to executives only.

In response to a question designed to establish whether executives thought that corporations would be required in the future to make social audits, 44 percent stated they thought such audits would be required.

Another study,[3] this one by a certified public accounting firm, analyzed social measurement disclosures in the annual reports of the Fortune 500 companies for the past three years. This compilation revealed that in 1971 there were 239 annual reports containing social measurement disclosures; in 1972 the number went up to 286; and in 1973 the disclosures had increased to 298.

Obviously, corporate social reporting is here and is increasing. Not only is this new development a response to the demands of consumer-activist groups and government regulatory bodies; but, as evidenced by the surveys reported above, business executives themselves recognize that such analysis has become a basic ingredient of effective management in today's social climate.

TYPES OF SOCIAL AUDITS

Recognition of the need for a social audit, however, does not imply universal corporate positive response. Inasmuch as surveys indicate there is no lack of interest on the part of the executives involved, why have companies not yet accepted a regular program of social reporting? What are the obstacles? In order to determine the impediments to the universal acceptance of social audits, 169 companies surveyed by the Committee for Economic Development were asked to rank in order of relative importance a number of specifically listed likely obstacles.[4]

Eighty-three companies reporting indicated the number one deterrent was the inability to develop measures of performance which everyone would accept. That is, about half of the companies stated that the lack of universal acceptance of measures of social performance was the principal obstacle to regularly preparing social audits.

What measures of social performance are being used by the many corporations already preparing social audits? They range from the simplistic inventorying of everything that a management itself considers a social activity to the rather sophisticated analyses involving the needs of society and the part the corporation plays in fulfilling those needs. For example, in General Electric Company, its strategic social planning and evaluation is built on a foundation of four major cornerstones: [5] social, political, economic, and technological. Included in its planning process is the development of a long-term environmental forecast. This is to establish the environmental assumptions upon which corporate marketing, manpower, technological, financial, and social strategies are to be based.

In another case, a leading food company initiated its own strategic planning with an ambitious corporationwide "social inventory." [6] The purpose of this information-gathering effort is to define in numerical terms what is being done, to spell out current social policies, and to clarify existing social goals. This is to "ascertain what we are now doing and to help us plan what progress we should expect in selected areas." The social inventory is viewed as an essential first step toward ongoing social audits, but stresses that the initial inventory is not intended for public disclosure. This would come later after much more experience. The company organized a "Social Audit Task Force" in the winter of 1972 to develop the inventory and to try to identify what society expects of the company. Significant impact areas were placed high on the list. In general, the inventory broke down into three major sectors: (1) public, (2) consumer, and (3) employee. Items under "public" included charitable giving, composition of the board of directors, recruiting of women and minorities, and ecology. Under "consumer," the topics listed included advertising, consumer complaints, product safety, packaging, and labeling. And the "employee" category included pay and fringe benefits, employee safety, and responding to the employee voice.

Among conclusions reached: The inventory was tougher to conduct than originally anticipated; definitions constituted a major problem, as did getting people to define the "social" part of their jobs. Particular difficulty was also experienced in splitting the "social" from the "good business" part of various activities, especially those in the consumer segment of the business.

One of the more confusing forms of social report was produced and distributed a couple of years ago by a management consulting firm to reflect its own activities. It was patterned after the conventional balance sheet and listed so-called social assets available and social commitments, obligations and equity. The exercise seemed unnecessarily cumbersome and complicated, and it was not clear what the significance of the results was supposed to be.

In a work by Harvard University's Raymond A. Bauer and Dan H. Fenn, [7] the social audit is portrayed as requiring executives to examine what they are doing and how they are doing it. This they call a *process audit* and set it forth in four basic steps: (1) Assess the circumstances under which each social program audited came into being; (2) spell out the program's goals; (3) explain the rationale involved, that is, how the company plans to attain the goals; (4) describe what is actually being done.

This kind of audit reflects only some of a company's social contributions and ignores its harmful social actions and nonactions. With militant monitoring groups and government agencies increasing in number, size, sophistication, and resolve, in my judgment we have no choice but to give visibility to both the pro and the con social activities. Increasingly, a gathering army of watchdogs is reporting corporate activities in their own terms and from their own frames of reference. Would a company not be better served by telling the truth in a creditable manner about its social actions, negative or positive, than by having uninformed reporters air the story for them?

One interesting example of a social audit program was conducted by A.R.A. Services, Inc., a $700 million enterprise engaged in institutional food services and a variety of merchandising operations.[8] In 1971, a committee was appointed to investigate how well the company was meeting its social responsibilities. The committee identified six major areas of corporate social responsibility: (1) employment and training;

(2) environment; (3) consumerism; (4) business concern; (5) provision of socially needed services; (6) fixing responsibility within the corporation.

Under employment and training, the basic premise was: "Business is increasingly expected to provide jobs and promotion opportunities, as the individual's merit dictates, to all the minorities who have historically met obstacles—the blacks, the longtime unemployed, women, the physically handicapped and exconvicts." It then went on to question how many disadvantaged should be found in a work force of a thousand people. How much and what kinds of training represent a conscionable offering? How many blacks, women, and others should be advanced, and to what degree in the hierarchy? Finally, it attempted to evaluate the company's performance in comparison with other companies. Similar observations and judgments were made in the other five areas.

A major thrust of Westinghouse Electric Corporation's social action program [9] was to pinpoint those areas where the company's advanced technological knowhow can be best applied to benefit society and the company simultaneously. Assumptions on both economic and social conditions were developed by seven top officers. Significant social problems were identified early and the conclusion reached that through close coordination with federal, state, and local government representatives, the company could make important contributions in the areas defined. At the same time it could boost its own growth and profits. An initial step was to isolate such specific high-potential targets as low-income housing and pollution control and apply technology to help solve the problems that exist.

SETTING THE STAGE

To successfully implement a social audit program, a company must be organizationally geared to the effort. It must prepare itself to set into motion corporate machinery to: (1) evaluate, quantitatively where possible, the social environment in which it functions; (2) establish improvement objectives; (3) make resource allocations in response to identified needs; (4) measure and evaluate coporate social involvement on an ongoing basis. However formidable this may seem, it is no more complicated than setting up the planning and support organization for a new product line or for a marketing or manpower development program.

Setting long- and short-range goals to achieve predetermined social gains will mean formulating procedures to deal with public and internal pressures, existing and anticipated legal restraints.

Many companies already embarked on social action programs attack the problem from two approaches: to eliminate the negative, that is, eliminate what they are doing that adversely affects the environment and society; and to accentuate the positive, that is, undertake social actions to improve the lifestyle and the environment.

It is ironic, but frequently some corporations which abuse the environment and humanity look quite good on their current profit-and-loss statements. Sophisticated analysts have always been aware that those managements which neglect their machinery and equipment and do not make expenditures to train junior executives often show higher earnings during the short term than is justified. In time, of course, this neglect of equipment and executive personnel training takes its toll in the operating effectiveness of the company.

In the same way, business management can show good operating profit results by ignoring the harm it is doing by dumping poisonous production waste into streams or polluting the atmosphere. In our present system of business reporting, we do not measure or include in any statement prepared by management, the damage done to a stream when the poisonous pollutants are dumped into it, or to the landscape when the land is scarred and mutilated by machine-efficient strip-mining techniques. Nor do we give proper reporting credit for the "good" that management does. Accountability for these pro and con social actions should not be ignored any longer.

It may be years before we can invent and use social measurement to evaluate social contributions with the confidence and relative precision with which we use economic and fiscal measurements. But we do have enough standards available in social areas so that we can begin now. However, considering the softness of much of the economic and fiscal data used today, as well as how these data often are misused, we could very well expect the results of social measurements, with all their present limitations, to be just as effective as economic measurements. What we can do at once is to borrow from economics and apply the "system" of economic and fiscal measurement to social areas.

Dollars involving social costs incurred by business are clearly determinable. The fact that a statement prepared of these costs may not be complete is not sufficient reason for us to delay further the preparation and use of such exhibits. In time, adequate guidelines will be developed.

SOCIOECONOMIC OPERATING STATEMENT (SEOS)

There is no legitimate reason why a social exhibit could not be prepared today along with a business organization's profit and loss statement and balance sheet. It could be a tabulation of those expenditures made *voluntarily* by a business aimed at improving the welfare of employees and public; safety of the product; and conditions of the environment. Such expenditures required by law or union contract need not be included, inasmuch as these are mandatory and thereby necessary costs of doing business.

There is a number of important observers who argue that creditable visibility should not be denied for positive social actions undertaken by a corporation even when they are mandated by law or contract. This could be accomplished within the format of the SEOS statement I propose by means of footnote presentation. We should recognize, however, that expenditures which are required by law or by contract are necessary costs of doing business, whether socially beneficial or not. Without such expenditures, a corporation could not continue in business.

Offset against these *pro bono publico* expenditures could be those costs of socially beneficial items which have been brought to the attention of management and which a "reasonable prudent socially aware management" would be expected to undertake, but this management chooses to ignore.

The statements themselves could be prepared by a small internal interdisciplinary team. Members of the team might include a seasoned business executive, sociologist, accountant, public health administrator, economist, or members of other disciplines whose specific expertise would apply to a particular industry or circumstance. They would then be audited by an outside independent interdisciplinary team.

The kind of specific items I am talking about to be included in such a tabulation are: cost of a training program for handicapped workers; cost of reclaiming and landscaping an old dump on company property; cost of installing pollution control devices on smokestacks; cost of detoxifying waste from finishing processes; cost of substituting leadfree paint for previously used poisonous lead paint.

The kind of items which would be picked up or charged against a business, much like contingent liabilities or deferrals are today, are costs which would have been incurred to re-landscape a strip-mining site used this year; estimated cost if there had been installed a purification process to neutralize poisonous liquid being dumped into a stream; cost of a safety device recommended by the Safety Council but not added to the product.

The basic guidelines for the SEOS follow: [10]

1. If a socially beneficial action is required by enforceable law or union regulations, it is not included in the SEOS.

2. If a socially beneficial action is required by law, but is ignored, the cost of such item is a DETRIMENT for the year. The same treatment is given an item if postponed, even with government approval.

3. A prorated portion of salaries and related expenses of personnel who spend time in socially beneficial actions or with social organizations is included.

4. Cash and product contributions to social institutions are included.

5. The cost of setting up facilities for the general good of employees or the public, if done voluntarily without union or government mandate, is included.

6. Expenditures made voluntarily for the installation of safety devices on the premises or in products and not required by law or other contract are included.

7. Neglecting to install safety devices to protect employees or the public, where available at reasonable cost, is a DETRIMENT.

8. The cost of voluntarily building a playground or nursery facility for employees and/or neighbors is included. Operating costs of the unit are also included for each succeeding year applicable.

9. The cost of re-landscaping strip-mining sites or other environmental eyesores, if not required by law, are included.

10. Extra costs of designing and building business facilities to upgrade health, beauty, or safety standards are included.

I am convinced that statements giving visibility to corporate social actions and nonactions will be required within the next ten years for most business organizations. These exhibits will be useful to internal managment as well as to consumer groups, special institutional investors, and an increasing number of regulatory governmental agencies. Even though this kind of exhibit may not yet be the total answer to full accountability for all corporate social responsibility, it would constitute a major step in that direction at this time.

Public visibility through a standardized Socioeconomic Operating Statement would act as a strong motivator for business executives and an equalizer as well, giving the socially responsible company as well as the laggard its due. Many organizations such as the Council on Economic Priorities, Ralph Nader's organizations, the United Church of Christ, Dreyfuss Third Century Fund, and Yale University are already attempting, but each in its own way, to identify and give visibility to social actions and nonactions of specific companies

Proposed Tax Credit

Congress should enact legislation allowing companies a deduction against taxable income for net social expenditures shown on the Socioeconomic Operating Statement for the year, which exceed a certain percentage of the taxpayer's net worth. I would recommend that such net socioeconomic expenditures, which exceed 1 percent of the net worth of a company, be allowed as a full deduction from taxable income. This would be in addition to all other expense and depreciation allowances already made for these same items. Such a tax allowance would consciously assert the collective responsibility for our environmental and social problems by having government and the citizen-consumer indirectly share in the costs.

ISSUES RAISED

The proposed SEOS has now been given exposure to the business, professional, and academic communities for over two years. Some companies have prepared such statements for internal purposes and experimented with them. Members of the accounting, management consulting, social science, political science, and journalism professions, among others, have analyzed and critiqued it. So have some government officials and financial analysts. Here are the principal issues raised:

(1) According to consumerists, an awesome array of corporate social actions should be taken that are not being taken. If some of the demands were complied with, it would all but bankrupt the company. How does one draw the line between social responsibility and corporate irresponsibility?

It is not an SEOS objective to pressure management into unreasonable social actions. In determining which programs to launch and which to discontinue, the company's interdisciplinary team would apply the "prudent man" principle of evaluation long used in the courts and in business decision making.

In responding to social needs and demands, a businessman would be expected to do what a reasonable, prudent, and socially concerned executive would do. The outside interdisciplinary committee would in turn apply the "prudent man" rule in objectively auditing the corporate social actions and omissions reported by the internal team.

The selection of social improvements and detriments to include in the SEOS would become less of a problem as experience is gained. Industry practice would be established through usage. Professional associations would help to set specific guidelines. In borderline situations, outside consultants might be called in to offer impartial and objective judgments. As corporate social disclosure expands throughout industry, precedents will be set.

(2) We can't expect a business executive to identify and report social detriments. Would he not resist disclosures that might hurt the company image?

Executive concern over negative revelations is an old story, witness the hue and cry that went up over SEC disclosure requirements four decades ago. As long as disclosure was applicable to competitors as well, no one was harmed. Further, negative self-exposure is not new to business. Companies always have made adverse financial conditions visible when they report contingent liabilities and set up reserves for litigation, bad debts, etc. The reality is that business disclosure is a fact with which we have to live. Increasing numbers of consumer-activist groups and investors are monitoring corporate social performance. These groups report what they find, sometimes from prejudiced points of view, and in terms designed to serve their ends. Since visibility will be given all social actions and nonactions by corporations, fair and balanced exposure would not be to the disadvantage of the sincere businessman.

(3) It will take years to develop the specific standards, indicators, and rules that will be needed for a full SEOS presentation.

If we wait for specific guidelines and rules that might be formulated for all diverse situations, it would be like waiting for all the nation's economists to agree on the guidelines and rules governing our economic presentations. General guidelines have been developed and promulgated for the SEOS.

We are faced with the choice of simplifying the issue or complicating it beyond practicality. Our objective is a social measurement tool to give visibility and to make period-by-period and company-by-company comparisons within an industry.

(4) What about potential revenues attributable to the program?

There is nothing gained by attempting to deduct projected profits from social contributions. Financial gains make social improvements none the less beneficial. The ultimate rules and guidelines we seek will be developed through a combination of usage and research.

(5) The SEOS handles a very complex evaluation procedure in quantitative, simplified terms. You can't always put a dollar price tag on all social actions.

In most social actions, a price tag is not difficult to arrive at if esoteric factors are avoided. Dollar expenditures for social improvements are what we are concerned with in the SEOS.

An example we might consider is the bank student loan program or ghetto loan program where applicants borrow at a reduced rate and on easy repayment terms. Costing such a program could be made very complex if we attempt to value and price tag all the ramifications involved.

Bernard L. Butcher of the Bank of America [11] has analyzed some of these ramifications: Future profits the bank might expect from new customers developed by the student loan program; the bank's and/or society's share of the benefits resulting from the increased income level of students who presumably would not have attended college without the loan; increased bank business resulting from the increment to the area's economy because of the improved educational level generated.

The alternative is a straight calculation of the difference between bank income received from student and ghetto loans and the payout from conventional loans.

CONCLUSIONS

The point we should keep in mind when attempting social measurement is not to expect more from statements setting forth social actions than we do from statements reflecting economic actions. The traditional profit-and-loss statement deals only with determinable income and cost. Esoteric matters such as values created by training manpower, potential benefits from research and development costs, "real" values of inventories, and unforeseen possible liabilities for product defects are not adequately considered in the preparation of the P & L statement, yet the statements are valuable tools in analyzing and comparing operating results.

Further, trying to determine the profit or loss of a business for an artificial period of one year in the complex life of a corporation could be considered to be so complicated as to be impossible. Yet, because of necessity we have learned to prepare and to use effectively annual profit-and-loss statements. Their use is meaningful in spite of their many weaknesses, especially for comparative purposes within a particular company for year-to-year evaluations, and for comparative purposes between companies. Why should we expect more from a social statement?

Perhaps I should note that all my remarks deal with micro-socioeconomic measurement as opposed to macro-socioeconomic measurement. The macro aspect concerns itself with the social measurement for an industry or a complete company. This dimension is for the attention of national governmental planning agencies. The micro dimension is concerned with the various activities of particular companies. This is something that individual managements can implement at any time.

I believe it was Oliver Wendell Holmes who stated, "We need elucidation of the obvious a good deal more than investigation of the obscure." Some form of social statement such as the Socioeconomic Operating Statement is an elucidation of the obvious in the area of corporate social responsiveness.

Stockholders and enlightened business executives should insist that there be no further delay in implementing a standardized reporting procedure for the social actions and nonactions of a business organization. It can be done now. To a large extent, the business enterprise dominates our society. Those responsible for directing the affairs of these mammoth institutions cannot be expected to initiate and expand activities which in their immediate impact adversely affect the profit-and-loss statement, thereby reflecting adversely on incumbent management's stewardship.

NOTES

1. *The Corporation in Transition* (Washington, D.C.: Chamber of Commerce of the U.S., 1973), pp. 45–47.
2. George A. Steiner, "What Is Business Doing About the Social Audit?" (New York: Committee for Economic Development, 1974).
3. Unpublished survey conducted by Ernst & Ernst (Cleveland, Ohio, Octooer 14, 1974).
4. Steiner, *op. cit.*
5. Ian H. Wilson, "Reforming the Strategic Planning Process." Paper prepared for NACBS symposium on social responsibility (Berkeley, Calif.: Graduate School of Business, University of California, November 9–11, 1972).
6. S. M. Hunt, "Conducting A Social Inventory," *Management Accounting* (October 1974).
7. Raymond A. Bauer and Dan H. Fenn, Jr., "What Is a Corporate Social Audit?" *Harvard Business Review* (January–February 1973).
8. John J. Carson, "A Corporate Social Audit?" *The Center Magazine* (January/February 1972).
9. Senator Frank E. Moss, *Initiatives in Corporate Responsibility* (Washington, D.C.: Consumer Subcommittee Report for Committee on Commerce, U.S. Senate, October 2, 1972).
10. Adapted from David F. Linowes, *The Corporate Conscience* (New York: Hawthorn Books, 1974).
11. Remarks by Bernard L. Butcher at Interdisciplinary Roundtable on Social Measurement, sponsored by American Institute of Certified Public Accountants (Charleston, South Carolina, April 5–7, 1972).

SEVEN

Responsibility
and Accountability
in American Medicine

Harry Schwartz

Visiting Professor of Medical Economics
Faculty of Medicine
Columbia University

As an intellectual experiment, let us begin by considering two conceivable opposite extremes of therapeutic practice. The first will be a model based upon recommendations of believers in maximum free enterprise; the second, upon recommendations of believers in maximum practicable total control.

In the first variant, we may think of a society in which anyone who wishes is freely permitted to set up shop and offer his services as a healer. Imagine a row of stores on an urban street, the first one occupied by a chiropractor, the second by a homeopathic physician, the third by an allopathic physician, the fourth by a naturopath, the fifth by a witch doctor, the sixth by an Iroquois medicine man, the seventh by a faith healer, the eighth by a religious science practitioner of one persuasion or another, the ninth by an expert in voodoo incantations, the tenth by an acupuncturist, and so on. In this model each of these self-licensed and self-designated therapists competes for the trade of the sick, the lame, and the halt.

Under this situation of open competition, the consumer has maximally free choice and so has the therapist. Presumably, over a long enough period of time, consumers would develop preferences based upon experience and some therapists would prosper because of their perceived performance efficacy and efficiency, while others would be compelled to shut up shop because of lack of trade. In such a model, we may suppose, there would be no need for any formal mechanisms to assure responsibility or accountability since consumers would quickly perceive differences in effectiveness among the competitive healers. The untrammeled competition would be relied upon to give results that in more constricted models might require formal governmental measures.

At the other extreme we may conceive of a medical system, perhaps attainable a few years or decades from now, which would require each self-designated sick person to present himself at a designated computer terminal complete with all possible computer-attached sensors and manipulative instruments. At this terminal a semiskilled attendant would have only the task of applying the various sensors and instruments to the appropriate portions of the patient's anatomy. Once applied these sensors and instruments would record and transmit to the computer's central processing unit all necessary information about the patient's condition, including all information needed to diagnose any disease. The central processing unit presumably would have all available medical knowledge and would be appropriately updated daily to assure that it was fully current with the latest scientific findings. For most patients, presumably, the computer would immediately supply a complete diagnosis plus an optimal therapeutic regimen, which might include the administration of appropriate drugs, the use of indicated operations or radiation therapy, etc. We may suppose that in this futuristic medical system all drugs, surgery, radiation, etc., are administered by computer-directed machines so that no problem of human negligence arises. At most, mechanical or electromechanical faults in the machinery might produce errors. But for these problems the computerized medical system might have maintenance computer systems that keep eternal watch and seek to prevent any malfunction.

Presumably in this future computerized utopia there might sometimes be patients who presented themselves with symptoms and internal data readings so discordant that no satisfactory diagnosis could be made by the central processor. In such cases, the recommended treatment might be provided by some appropriate random-choice mechanism. But in all cases where diagnosis was possible, the patient could be confident that he had received the best care that was computerly possible. In this system, too, presumably, problems of responsibility and accountability would be minimal.

In the real world in which we all live, of course, there is neither completely free competition nor is there any recognized single fount of knowledge. Instead we have a situation of considerable competition, considerable effort at government regulation and control which some might argue is moving toward the computer extreme outlined above, and considerable but by no means complete knowledge about illness and means of treating it.

With the avowed aim of protecting the consumer, government has limited competition in the hope of limiting risk. Thus, medical practitioners must be licensed by the state and the practice of medicine without a license is a crime. But chiropractors also are licensed, though their therapeutic competence is a matter of considerable dispute. Moreover, it is common observation that many unlicensed therapists are at work, often profitably. One may receive therapeutic advice from pharmacists; from advertisements on radio and television and in the print media; from self-designated experts in nutrition, acupuncture, religious healing, and the like; as well as from one's neighbors. It is always amazing to me personally to find so many people who are convinced of such "facts" as the efficacy of copper bracelets against rheumatism and the indispensability of massive doses of vitamins to vigor and longevity. I am even more amazed by those academic critics of conventional medicine who believe that medicine has an effective monopoly of therapy and that patients behave like puppets in obeying physicians.

Nevertheless, we shall focus here on conventional medicine, not because it has a monopoly of therapeutic activity, but because it is the largest single element in the nation's therapy "nonsystem" and because we have the most information in this area. One hears rumors, for example, of Christian Scientists who stray from the fold and consult physicians rather than Christian Science readers, but there seem to be no systematic statistics kept on such matters.

The existing structure of conventional medicine is one in which extensive competition coexists with extensive regulation. If an individual requires open heart surgery—say, perhaps, the replacement of his aortic valve—he can go to Dr. Michael DeBakey in Texas, Dr. Norman Shumway in California, and no doubt several thousand other surgeons who offer themselves as competent to perform this procedure. Drs. DeBakey, Shumway *et al.* compete in a framework defined by a large body of law. They must, as we have noted before, be licensed to practice medicine and surgery. Many of their assistants—for example, registered nurses—must also be licensed. The physicians' choice of drugs is regulated by the Food and Drug Administration, and at any given time there are drugs routinely being employed in other countries which may not legally be prescribed in the United States because they have not received FDA approval. The hospitals in which these surgeons operate are subject to inspection and approval or disapproval by the Joint Commission on Accreditation of Hospitals. There are numerous other agencies which inspect and regulate; for example, fire departments keep an eye on and attempt to minimize fire hazards, local health departments seek to guard against food-borne epidemics in hospitals, etc.

THE ROLE OF MALPRACTICE LAWS

Despite this plethora of licenses, rules, regulations, inspectors, and the like, every participant in the conventional medical system knows that his responsibility and accountability to each patient is ultimately defined by the law of malpractice as that law is implemented in constantly changing fashion by the courts of the various states. The *Random House Dictionary of the English Language* informs us that malpractice is the "failure of a professional person to render proper services through reprehensible ignorance or negligence, or through criminal

intent, esp. when injury or loss follows." Not surprisingly, the dictionary example of the word's use is "the malpractice of a physician."

This is not the place to attempt to give a detailed legal analysis of the
meaning and application of the malpractice concept. But some com-
mentary about this blanket effort at consumer protection seems war-
ranted. The malpractice concept gives no guarantee that a physician
will always be correct and certainly no guarantee that he can always
effect a cure. But at a minimum, the right of a suit against malpractice
seeks to assure three fundamental protections: (1) the physician has not
acted with criminal intent, for example, by killing or disabling a
patient for personal gain; (2) the physician has applied some generally
satisfactory standard of knowledge and competence in considering the
case—though the definition of such a standard has been a matter of
considerable litigation; and (3) the physician has not been guilty of
negligence; if a surgeon he has not left any instruments or sponges in
the patient's abdomen; if an internist he has not omitted some essential
test required to reach a correct diagnosis; etc.

At this late date, there is no need to treat at length the importance
malpractice has assumed in American medicine. A rising level of court
cases and a rising level of maximum damage awards—some of them in
the millions of dollars—have combined to create a substantial economic problem. Physicians now find the availability of malpractice
insurance is no longer to be taken for granted as losses force various
insurance companies to withdraw from the field. Moreover, malpractice insurance has been one of the most inflationary items in a generally
inflationary economy. That a neurosurgeon or anesthesiologist may
have to pay between $10,000 and $20,000 a year for malpractice
insurance is no longer a matter of surprise. In the spring of 1975,
skyrocketing malpractice insurance costs led a number of states to
enact legislation designed to hold them down.

Even more worrisome are the assertions that physicians more and
more tend to practice "defensive medicine," that is, to order only
marginally necessary X-ray or other examinations and to call in only
marginally necessary consultants because they wish to have maximum
protection should they be sued for malpractice. Attorneys representing
malpractice claimants have a different view, of course, arguing that
only a small fraction of actual malpractice is represented by litigation

and defending malpractice suits a powerful instrument for improving the quality of medical care delivered to patients.

Whatever one's views in the current controversies regarding malpractice, there can be no question about the potency of this legal instrument for constantly reminding physicians of their responsibility and accountability to their patients. What is remarkable at the present time, however, is the ongoing creation of a new and more comprehensive instrument for responsibility and accountability, the federally legislated Professional Standards Review Organizations (PSRO) provided for by Section 249F of Public Law 92-603, the so-called Bennett Amendment.

BALOONING OF GOVERNMENT COSTS

In the judgment of many observers, PSRO's introduction is the most important change in the American medical system in many years, a change whose full impact or potential it is impossible to overestimate. The roots of PSRO are to be found in the Social Security Amendments of 1965, particularly Titles XVIII and XIX which provided for the creation of Medicare and Medicaid. These are the laws under which the government finances much of the medical care now received by the elderly and the indigent. The monetary effects of these new programs can be stated briefly. In fiscal year 1965, all levels of government paid for less than $7 billion of the total personal health-care expenditures in the United States, roughly 20.8 percent. In fiscal year 1972, the total governmental expenditure for this purpose was almost $27 billion, or 37.2 percent.[1] This vast spending continued to rise sharply. The rapid and dizzying growth of these expenditures had not been expected. By the early 1970s, expenditures for Medicare alone, for example, were rapidly approaching twice the amounts that had originally been projected during the congressional debates.[2]

As a result, the search was on for the culprits responsible for this massive overexpenditure of government funds. It could not, of course, be conceded that the original legislation had been faulty, and it was politically impossible to remedy the problems by cutting back seriously on the generosity of the medical aid entitlements, especially to the Medicare beneficiaries, all of whom are potential voters. The focus quickly shifted, therefore, to exposés of abuses by providers of medical care. And in a nation of over 200 million persons it was not difficult to find examples of such abuse. Soon congressional hearings informed the people and Congress about physicians and other providers who charged for excessive and unnecessary services. With the culprits so defined, the answer to the problem seemed clear enough. What was needed, apparently, was some sort of police system to supervise the delivery of medical care paid for by the government, both to discourage abuses and to catch and punish those who were guilty.

SEARCH FOR A MEDICAL POLICE FORCE

The first step aimed at creating such a medical police system was apparently taken by the Nixon administration in October 1969. This was done by offering a so-called Health Cost Effectiveness bill. This bill proposed to create "program review teams" (PRT) composed of physicians, other health professionals, and consumer representatives appointed by the Secretary of Health, Education, and Welfare. The bill envisaged that these teams would review the quality and quantity of services provided under Medicare and provide information on the basis at which the Secretary of HEW could make ineligible for Medicare reimbursement any physicians found to be overcharging or providing excessive or inferior services.[3]

The American Medical Association did not like the idea of creating this medical police force and began casting about for ways to avoid this situation. Here is how the AMA later described the situation it faced:[4]

In March 1970, representatives of the Association met with members of the House Ways and Means Committee and, in June 1970, with members of the Senate Finance Committee. Both Committees expressed the strong concern of Congress about the increasing cost of Medicare and Medicaid, and about allegations that physicians and other providers were providing unneeded services and otherwise abusing the program. Leaders of both Committees expressed their strong interest in control of such abuses by an effective, structured peer review program developed and operated by physicians and medical societies, and they urged the Association to prepare and present such a plan.

To meet this request, the AMA in 1970 came up with the idea of what it called a Peer Review Organization which would have the Secretary of HEW contract with state medical societies for performance of peer review. The resulting PRO amendment was endorsed at the 1970 annual AMA convention. In May 1970, the House of Representatives passed a bill including the "program review team" approach. And in August 1970, Senator Wallace Bennett introduced a Professional Standards Review Organization (PSRO) amendment which he claimed gave the medical profession what it wanted except for review through state medical associations.

The ensuing political maneuvering need not concern us here except to note that when Public Law 92-603 (earlier referred to as H.R.-1) was signed into law on October 30, 1972 it contained both section 249F, providing for Senator Bennett's PSRO, and section 229, providing for Program Review Teams. In effect, the secretary of HEW was given two separate, potentially duplicating or complementary mechanisms for checking on medical services provided in accordance with government programs such as Medicare and Medicaid. This discussion will focus on PRSO, but it should not be forgotten that the Program Review Teams are also in the law and that in the second half of 1974 proposed regulations governing Program Review Teams appeared in the Federal Register. Conceivably PRTs could in the future supersede PSRO as the chief government mechanism for checking on medicine. It should be noted that in the minds of many skeptical observers, PSRO—though hotly assailed by many in organized medicine—is seen as representing an undue set of concessions to doctors, as putting foxes to guard the chickenhouse. The populist-minded Senator Fred R. Harris enunciated this latter point of view when he declared in late 1970 that PRSO "grants organized medicine too much control over utilization of facilities and payment of claims."

GOALS OF PROFESSIONAL STANDARDS
REVIEW ORGANIZATION

The goal of PSRO is accurately stated in the declaration of purpose contained in section 1151 of section 249F:

In order to promote the effective, efficient, and economical delivery of health care services of proper quality for which payment may be made (in whole or in part) under this Act and in recognition of the interests of patients, the public, practitioners, and providers in improved health care services, it is the purpose of this part to assure, through the application of suitable procedures of professional standards review, that the services for which payment may be made under the Social Security Act will conform to appropriate professional standards for the provision of health care and that payment for such services will be made—
(1) only when, and to the extent, medically necessary, as determined in the exercise of reasonable limits of professional discretion; and
(2) in the case of services provided by a hospital or other health care facility on an inpatient basis, only when and for such period as such services cannot, consistent with professionally recognized health care standards, effectively be provided on an outpatient basis or more economically in an inpatient health care facility of a different type, as determined in the exercise of reasonable limits of professional discretion.

Even this brief statement of purpose makes plain the essence of PSRO. It is an attempt to impose accountability upon physicians, accountability primarily to the government with respect to services for which it pays. The government wants to pay only for services that are "medically necessary as determined in the exercise of reasonable limits of professional discretion." And it wants the services it pays for to be delivered in the least expensive setting possible, again, "as determined in the exercise of reasonable limits of professional discretion."

What is "medically necessary"? What are the "reasonable limits of professional discretion"? On the face of the matter, these are extraordinarily vague terms susceptible of the most varied interpretations. One need not be a lawyer to see the abundant opportunities such language gives for disagreements and therefore probably ultimately for litigation in the courts.

To accomplish its purposes, this legislation authorizes the setting up of Professional Standards Review Organizations intended to cover the entire United States, each one covering an area defined by the Secretary of HEW. Each organization is to be made up of licensed doctors of medicine or osteopathy engaged in the practice of medicine or surgery in its geographical area. If more than 10 percent of an area's doctors object to a proposed PSRO, the Secretary of HEW must poll the physicians of the area involved and abide by the decision of a majority of such voters as to whether or not he shall contract with a given organization. If, by January 1, 1976, the Secretary is unable in any area or areas to contract with an organization such as that described above for review purposes in that area, he may thereafter contract with some other organization to do this work.

What this amounts to, of course, is a threat. If in any specific PSRO area local physicians refuse to form and approve a review organization then the Secretary of HEW is entitled after January 1, 1976, to turn to some other group—a nearby medical school or school of public health, a local or state department of health, an insurance company, or some ad hoc commercial organization formed solely for this purpose—to perform this review. What this provision says in effect is that if local doctors will not review each other, the government will empower other people to do the reviewing it wants.

The functions of a PSRO are defined in section 1155 of the legislation we are considering. The key portions of this section are presented below:

Sec. 1155 (a) (1) Notwithstanding any other provision of law, but consistent with the provisions of this part, it shall (subject to the provisions of subsection (g)) be the duty and function of each Professional Standards Review Organization for any area to assume, at the earliest date practicable, responsibility for the review of the professional activities in such area of physicians and other health care practitioners and institutional and noninstitutional providers of health care services in the provision of health care services and items for which payment may be made (in whole or in part) under this Act for the purpose of determining whether—

(A) such services and items are or were medically necessary;

(B) the quality of such services meets professionally recognized standards of health care; and

(C) in case such services and items are proposed to be provided in a hospital or other health care facility on an inpatient basis, such services and items could, consistent with the provision of appropriate medical care, be effectively provided on an outpatient basis or more economically in an inpatient health care facility of a different type.

(2) Each Professional Standards Review Organization shall have the authority to determine, in advance, in the case of—

(A) any elective admission to a hospital, or other health care facility, or

(B) any other health care service which will consist of extended or costly courses of treatment,

whether such service, if provided, or if provided by a particular health care practitioner or by a particular hospital or other health care facility, organization, or agency, would meet the criteria specified in clauses (A) and (C) of paragraph (1).

(3) Each Professional Standards Review Organization shall, in accordance with the regulations of the Secretary, determine and publish, from time to time, the types and kinds of cases (whether by type of health care of diagnosis involved, or whether in terms of other relevant criteria relating to the provision of health care services) with respect to which such organization will in order most effectively to carry out the purposes of this part, exercise the authority conferred upon it under paragraph (2).

(4) Each Professional Standards Review Organization shall be responsible for the arranging for the maintenance of and the regular review of profiles of care and services received and

provided with patient profiles, methods of coding which will provide maximum confidentiality as to patient identity and assure objective evaluation consistent with the purposes of this part. Profiles shall also be regularly reviewed on an ongoing basis with respect to each health care practitioner and provider to determine whether the care and services ordered or rendered are consistent with the criteria specified in clauses (A), (B), and (C) of paragraph (1).

Paragraph (e) of section 1155 provides that each PSRO "shall utilize the services of, and accept the findings of, the review committees of a hospital or other operating health care facility or organization located in the area served by such organization but only when and only to the extent and only for such time that such committees in such hospital or other operating health care facility or organization have demonstrated to the satisfaction of such organization their capacity effectively and in timely fashion to review activities in such hospital or other operating health care facility" to accomplish the purposes of the act.

Section 1156 (a) provides that each PSRO "shall apply professionally developed norms of care, diagnosis, and treatment based upon typical patterns of practice in its regions (including typical lengths-of-stay for institutional care by age and diagnosis) as principal points of evaluation or review." Paragraph (b) of this section provides that

such norms with respect to treatment for particular illnesses or health conditions shall include (in accordance with regulations of the Secretary)—

(1) the types and extent of the health care services which, taking into account differing, but acceptable, modes of treatment and methods of organizing and delivering care are considered within the range of appropriate diagnosis and treatment of such illness or health condition, consistent with professionally recognized and accepted patterns of care;

(2) the type of health care facility which is considered consistent with such standards, to be the type in which health care services which are medically appropriate for such illness or condition can most economically be provided.

PLANNED ROLE OF PSRO

Against this background of extracts from the legislation, we can now attempt to summarize more simply the planned operation of PSROs. In effect, every physician has been placed on notice that the government intends to review the services he provides to patients for whom the government pays the bill. Initially, this review will be confined to hospital and nursing-home care. But eventually this review will include all care, including care given in physicians' private offices.

Each area's PSRO will do the reviewing, using local physicians, except that hospitals and other installations may be allowed to review themselves if they prove to have that capacity. The review will essentially take the following form: For each diagnosis—and there has been talk of norms for some 350 diseases—there will be a statement of proper workup (permissible tests, etc.) and treatment. There will also be a statement of the permissible range of hospital stay.

The possibility that PSROs will require advance permission for "elective admission to a hospital, or other health care facility" or for "any other health care service which will consist of extended or costly courses of treatment" is explicitly provided for in the law, as we have seen above. But present HEW policy is to minimize fear that such prior permission will be required. Thus, Deputy Assistant Secretary for Health Dr. Henry E. Simmons, director, Office of Professional Standards Review at HEW, wrote recently:

Such a policy of mandatory preadmission certification is neither mandated by the law nor advocated by the Office of Professional Standards Review. PSROs will be required to assess the necessity for and appropriateness of hospital admission on a concurrent basis. This must be done within one working day following the patient's admission to a hospital. Although concurrent admission certification initially will be required for all elective admissions, over time the PSRO may identify physicians, diagnoses (or problems), and/or institutions which no longer require such certification to prevent the delivery of inappropriate health care services.[5]

Nevertheless, the provisions remain in the law and we shall return to the possibilities they open. In any case, when the PSRO mechanism is fully functioning, the government will not pay for any services (by physician, hospital, nursing home, etc.) that is not approved by a local PSRO. Moreover, any physician or other provider may be denied eligibility to provide reimbursable services if he has "demonstrated an unwillingness or a lack of ability substantially to comply" with the law, or the provider may be fined by an amount up to $5000 as a condition for remaining eligible to provide reimbursable services (section 1160).

For laymen it seems useful to provide an example of the norms, criteria, and standards applicable to a given disease and a specific surgical procedure. As our example we shall take appendicitis followed by appendectomy, that is, removal of the diseased appendix. As our basis we shall employ a guidelines worksheet prepared by the American College of Surgeons for possible PSRO use.[6]

Appendectomy Under PSRO

Appendicitis is suspected and may justify hospital admission when a patient suffers abdominal pain and tenderness, especially if he has had previous attacks of discomfort which have been identified as appendicitis. A patient may remain in the hospital for two days for observation even if he is not operated upon. If he does have an appendectomy, his hospital stay may last three to seven days, if the appendix did not rupture before removal, or the stay may be seven to fourteen days if the appendix had ruptured before removal.

When appendicitis is suspected the physician may validly take a history of the patient and perform a physical examination with emphasis upon the abdomen, rectal, and pelvic examinations, and attention to fever, pulse, and state of hydration. (All such detailed spelling out, of course, is needed to justify each element of a physician's billing for his care.) After the appendix is removed, it is required that the tissue be submitted for examination to a pathologist who can determine whether it was diseased or not. Additionally, before the operation a patient suspected of having appendicitis usually has a complete blood count and a urinalysis, while he may also have a chest X-ray, an abdominal X-ray, an electrocardiogram (if the patient is over 45), a blood biochemical profile and determination of the blood's sedimentation rate and prothrombin time. In special cases, it may be deemed advisable to have an intravenous pyelogram, a barium enema, and a gastrointestinal series, all of these being X-ray examinations.

The operation and its sequellae may require consultations, special therapeutic services, and specific nursing services, depending upon the facts of the case. The physician may wish to administer sedatives, analgesics, narcotics, intravenous fluids, and antibiotics depending upon his patient's needs. The actual operation may be an appendectomy or a simple abdominal drainage procedure, or both. During the hospital stay, the surgeon will watch the patient's progress with special attention to wound healing, fever, and gastrointestinal function. He may encounter such important postoperative complications as sepsis and intestinal obstruction.

The patient may be discharged when he is ambulatory, free of fever, has no more significant wound drainage, and has a suitable home or other facility to which he can go for continued care. The physician is justified in having the patient return on an ambulatory basis for follow-up visits during a period of up to twenty-eight days after discharge.

Complexity of Disease Patterns

One has only to read the PSRO legislation to see that Congress was convinced that a case of appendicitis such as discussed above is the typical medical case, i.e., that typically there is one well-defined disease, that its treatment is well known and essentially stereotyped, and that therefore abuses in the way of departures from the norm can be easily detected. As a matter of fact, much of the discussion of the implementation of PSRO assumes that a great deal of it can be done by computer with the help of nurses. Only relatively infrequently, it is assumed, will problems involving the serious intervention of physician reviewers arise. Thus, in a case of appendicitis, a physician who ordered a brain scan would immediately fall under suspicion of abusing the system, as would a physician who tried to keep his appendectomy patient in the hospital for a month or longer.

Obviously, there are many cases where a simple situation such as appendicitis in a healthy young person arises and is adequately covered by the assumptions behind PSRO. But what about the cases which are not covered by these assumptions—especially the cases of elderly Medicare recipients who have multiple complaints in an almost infinite variety of possible combinations? Here is the way these problems are seen by a physician actively engaged in work with elderly Medicare recipients:

Principally, these problems arise from the sociomedical complexity of disease, especially as it occurs in elderly beneficiaries of the Social Security Act. It is the biology of the situation that confounds our schemes and hopes for demarcated parcels of care. The morbidity of the elderly accounts for about one third of crucial hospital care and the major part of the federal investment in it. The character of this morbidity far exceeds the simplistic models for determination of eligibility and criteria of care that have been presented so far. As one who has been professionally involved in various phases of care of the elderly for a number of years, I am not at all reassured by the common use of acute appendicitis to work out criteria and norms of care. Multiple, active pathological findings are the rule not the exception in hospital care of the elderly. In a statistical and clinical study published 11 years ago in *Lancet,* three of us in Scotland reported on the number of diseases (not subproblems or symptoms) presented by elderly patients entering a hospital geriatric unit. The women had a mean of almost six, the men, a mean of five diseases per patient and most of the diseases had some active bearing on disability and need for care. . . .

The concentration on the single diagnosis as a yardstick of care of the elderly has, therefore, to be one of the more outrageous anachronisms for medicine in 1974. It will be exceedingly important in the early phase of building up computer experience that data processing get wise to (or get "blown" by) the realities of multiproblem illness in the elderly. For this reason, my own institution does not supply "main" or principal diagnosis, but multiproblem lists to fiscal intermediaries, in an effort to resist the tendency to collapse the clinical dimensions for the convenience of the accounting or fiscal process.[7]

For the author of the above quotation—and probably for the great majority of physicians—PSRO is primarily and almost exclusively a penny-pinching effort to save money backed by punitive sanctions. The official line, however, is quite different. Thus, Dr. Henry E. Simmons, director of HEW's Office of Professional Standards Review, has recently written:

The major thrust of the PSRO program is education: the detection of problems in health care through peer review and the correction of those problems. This will be accomplished by a variety of measures, with the punitive provisions in the legislation used only as a last resort. Both physician and non-physician health care practitioners will be responsible for developing mechanisms by which the results of review are utilized in the continuing education of their peers to improve the quality of care they provide.[8]

Other Problems Under PSRO

Other problems with the review procedure can also be envisioned rather easily. For example, there is the well-known fact that for some medical conditions there is no known therapy—as in the case of multiple sclerosis. In other cases, there are widely divergent views about optimal therapy. In September 1974, when President Ford's wife, Betty, was operated on for breast cancer, this last matter came vividly into focus. Mrs. Ford was treated with a radical mastectomy after a malignant tumor was found in her breast, i.e., the surgeon removed not only the affected breast but also muscles and other surrounding tissue in a wide-ranging effort to remove parts of the breast area that might harbor disseminated cancer cells. But two days after the First Lady's operation, a National Cancer Institute announcement asserted that research had found to date that a less radical procedure, the so-called modified radical mastectomy, was equally efficacious against breast cancer.[9]

The debate between the two schools of thought on this matter has been prolonged and bitter, and the National Cancer Institute announcement by no means ended the argument. Will PSRO attempt to enunciate one mode of surgery for breast cancer and enforce its decision by means of its power to pay or withhold payment for services to Medicare and Medicaid recipients? The explosive possibilities here are obvious, but they cannot be dismissed as out of the question. After all, there are some who argue that the best therapy for breast cancer is the so-called lumpectomy, an even more modest and limited surgical procedure than the modified radical mastectomy. And some advocates of lumpectomy have charged at times that surgeons prefer to do the more extensive operations because they get more money for wide-ranging and time-consuming surgery than for limited procedures that can be done more rapidly.

Similar problems arise also in many other cases; for example, the use of noninsulin preparations for treating adult diabetics who have mild diabetes that cannot be controlled by diet alone. There are some experimental data suggesting the use of these preparations may raise the heart attack rate among users, yet many of the country's outstanding diabetologists insist these preparations provide sufficient benefit to justify any additional risk their ingestion may create. Such examples could be multiplied many times because medicine is not yet an exact science and there are profound and unresolved disputes about therapy among skilled physicians.

Then there is the problem of innovations. PSRO procedures assume the existence of one or a few permissible modes of treatment, and the aim of PSRO reviews is to rule out nonpermissible modes of treatment. But what if a physician (or a group of physicians) wishes to introduce a new technique that is not approved? Is he to be punished monetarily for the attempt at innovation, and if so will PSRO become a barrier to further technical progress in medical therapeutics? PSRO officials, of course, deny any such intent, and there is no reason to doubt their sincerity. Yet, in the nature of the case, any procedure which reviews medical care in the light of predetermined approved methodologies must inevitably exercise a conservative influence since it puts an additional barrier before those who would introduce change.

Additionally, it was pointed out earlier that the PSRO law provides that PSROs may require precertification for hospital admission and also for "any other health care service which will consist of extended or costly courses of treatment" (section 1155 (a) (2) (B)). The potentials are great for these precertification procedures to become mechanisms for the rationing of health care, and perhaps for cutting down the amount of health care to meet budgetary restrictions.

In mid-1974, for example, this writer visited the New Mexico Professional Standards Review Organization in Albuquerque, New Mexico, a pioneer in applying PSRO-type review procedures. Officials there explained how their review worked in the case of Medicaid recipients who are being treated by physicians belonging to the New Mexico Health Care Foundation. It was explained that the liberality of the Foundation in allowing certain types of treatment depends upon the budgetary situation. In a tight budgetary situation, it was explained, procedures and treatments are disallowed for which payment would be permitted when the budgetary situation was less stringent. In short, review was being used as a means of rationing medical care.

These possibilities are particularly serious because of the indications that the United States will have national health insurance in the not too distant future and that PSRO will be a component control mechanism in such a program. Many naive advocates have assumed that health insurance would provide all the medical care one would wish on demand. But since national health insurance will have a limited budget, it seems more likely that procedures will be used to limit care—especially expensive care such as heart transplants or complex and expensive types of surgery for some types of cancer, etc.

At another level of care entirely, it is well known that much ambulatory medical care is essentially the provision of reassurance and the supply of placebos, such as injections of vitamin B12. In New Mexico, this writer found that the review mechanism had already made plain it would not pay for injections of vitamin B12 or for other similar provisions of placebos. This saved money, but did it help make medical care more useful for the frightened and the disturbed who make up so large a proportion of the daily flow of the primary physician's patients?

PSRO and Privacy

Finally, there is the issue of privacy. Understandably this is one problem that PSRO proponents and officials have tended to minimize. They have argued that at present, with so much medical care paid for by third-party payers, medical privacy is a myth since patients' charts are handled by many hands in hospitals and in the third-party payment mechanisms.

There is certainly a substantial portion of truth in the argument made by these PSRO supporters, and there is no need to doubt their protestations that PSROs will attempt to maximize the protection they give to the confidentiality of materials they review. Yet the fact must be faced that inherent in the PSRO concept is the planned, systematic and required collection of the most sensitive type of information about all individuals now receiving Medicare, Medicaid, and maternal health benefits from the government, and that in the future PSRO will collect health data on all Americans served by a national health insurance scheme. One has only to recall the national indignation at the "plumbers'" effort to steal information about Daniel Ellsberg from his psychiatrist's office to comprehend the possibilities here.

Protestations of government officials that they plan to protect patients' privacy must be suspect simply from memories of official access to income tax records and of how easy it was for the press to get the original data about President Nixon's income tax returns from the government computer's memory. If the income tax payments of a President of the United States could not be protected from prying eyes, what reason is there to suppose that it will be possible to protect data about ordinary citizens who may have syphilis, have undergone an

abortion, or have secured treatment for a disease about which they
would rather others did not know?

Here is the way the *New York Times* expressed its concern about
government invasion of privacy via the computer—an invasion taking
place in many other fields besides medicine:

> The American capacity to collect and to store information
> about individuals and the American tendency to express ineffec-
> tual alarm at that development have grown enormously in the last
> decade and a half. Unfortunately, Congress' ability to develop
> legislation safeguarding the individual's right to privacy has
> lagged far behind computer technology. The nation is left with a
> vague sense that information monsters inevitably threaten to
> transform the society in which we live. . . .
>
> The initiation of new information-keeping systems is rarely
> inhibited by concern over their potential for invasion of privacy
> because they are usually established as aids to achievement of
> some private or governmental goal which is deemed desirable in
> itself.[10]

This *New York Times* editorial made no mention of PSRO, which
is certainly an information-keeping system established to aid
"achievement of some private or governmental goal which is deemed
desirable in itself." *The Wall Street Journal,* usually at the opposite
ideological pole from the *Times,* has commented in a similar vein which
is also appropriate to any consideration of PSRO and confidentiality: [11]

> . . . increasing government regulation and more government
> benefit programs have resulted in less privacy enjoyed by in-
> dividuals who live under that government.
>
> What this amounts to is a reaffirmation of the classical liberal
> doctrine that government participation necessarily involves some
> degree of government control, while extensive government par-
> ticipation involves extensive control. Yet there has been almost no
> sustained public discussion about the effects of government ac-
> cretion. Even now, when the lengths to which big government can

go are clear for all to see, discussions about the lack of privacy usually focus on individual excesses while ignoring the pattern that makes such excesses possible and perhaps even inevitable. . . .

It remains true that a government big enough to do things for you is big enough and usually ready and willing, to do things to you.

The potentials for breaching privacy became clear to me on that New Mexico visit mentioned above. There I was shown computer profiles on patients and physicians of the sort required by the PSRO law. For every lover of privacy these profiles can only be termed terrifying. Just by punching a few keys in a console keyboard, an operator could exhibit on a cathode-ray tube the entire medical care an individual had received during the entire period of the existence of this surveillance program. Similarly, by punching another set of keys one could get the physician profile, a complete and itemized list of all procedures, injections, diagnoses, etc., performed by the physician in question and submitted by him for payment. The thought could not be avoided that the computer had gone George Orwell one better. The novelist had imagined a world in 1984 in which Big Brother kept a television eye on everyone's activities. But the PRSO-type computer effort keeps an eye on and remembers all of one's medical care in detail, or, if one is a provider, all of the medical care one has administered to all of one's patients.

PSRO—A SUMMARY OF PROBLEMS

Perhaps by this time society's dilemma is clear. The form of accountability aimed at by PSRO seems justifiable enough at first glance. After all, the government should not be cheated by physicians or anyone else doing needless or excessive procedures in order to get paid from the public treasury. So a procedure is devised to try to stop such cheating, a procedure whose great expense and enormous effort make plain the assumption that the cheating to be stopped is on a grand scale. PSRO has been set in motion, and hundreds of millions of dollars will be spent on it just in the years immediately ahead. If national health insurance is passed soon, PSRO will control every American's medical care.

PSRO requires the effort to define every important illness and to define what is legitimate and what is illegitimate in the treatment of each illness. The complexities here are self-evident when one remembers the enormous variety of illnesses, the fact that an individual can have two or more illnesses and disabilities simultaneously, the truism that there is no standard therapy for many diseases while for others there are legitimate and deep differences among physicians as to appropriate treatment. Moreover, every setting down of acceptable norms of treatment immediately implies that all other treatments are not acceptable, including new treatments that may be more efficacious than those already approved. Finally, the vast effort to impose financial accountability upon American medicine requires the accumulation of huge computerized data banks on illness and treatment in America, data banks with vast potentials for intrusions on individual privacy.

Little wonder that this effort has encountered so much resistance from the American medical profession, resistance that is by no means over. And if the American Medical Association in June 1974 appeared to surrender on this issue, it was only because it was faced with evidence that continued resistance was useless and the government had even stronger means than PSRO of controlling medical care it paid for. So the experiment will take place at great cost, and all Americans must hope that the fears expressed above and elsewhere will prove ill-founded.

THE QUALITY OF MEDICAL CARE

Yet it would seem inappropriate for a layman to conclude a discussion of this extraordinarily important matter without giving a concrete example of the fears that crowd many physicians' minds. Let us con-

clude this essay with a statement by one of the nation's most distin-
guished surgeons, Professor Francis D. Moore of Harvard Medical
School, the chief surgeon of Peter Bent Brigham Hospital in Boston.
Here at some length is his nightmare vision of what may happen under
PSRO: [12]

A 45-year-old woman wishes to have a hysterectomy because of
recurrent vaginal bleeding from a small submucous fibroid. The
"normalized" hospital stay for a hysterectomy is 8.4 days. Certain
laboratory tests and examinations are required and acceptable. If
these conditions are met, the surgeon and the physician are paid
and so is the hospital. But we still have no idea of whether or not
the hysterectomy was really needed. Would she be better off just
to await the natural menopause? We have no idea whether or not
the inevitable urethral catheterization emptied the bladder but
filled it with *Escherichia coli,* leading to persistent pyelonephritis.
We are not told whether or not the laboratory "norms" contained
an adequate screen to determine that her anemia was actually
pernicious anemia rather than blood loss. And certainly we have
no idea as to whether or not the patient and her husband understood clearly what was being advised and what was involved. We
have no concept of whether or not the anesthetist was competent
to introduce the endotracheal tube without injuring the vocal
cords, whether or not an adequate allergic history of prior an-
esthetics was taken before administering a drug such as halothane
to the point of deep coma. We have no concept as to whether or
not the scrub nurses that day were a little careless and brought
instruments into the operating room from the one next door where
an abcess was being drained. In short, all the elaborate PSRO
conditions were met, but we have gained no insight into the
quality of the patient's care.

Moreover, when the patient did get ready to go home after 8.4
days, the surgeon still felt that she was a little weak and wobbly
and should not really go home quite yet. He was a little worried
about her strength. Her pulse was still elevated, even though the
electrocardiogram appeared to be normal. Looking over his rule
book for PSRO, he could find no identifiable complication that

would justify her further stay in the hospital. If he asked her to stay on for a day or two, neither he nor the hospital would be paid. The patient would have to pay out of her own pocket. There would always be the slight suspicion that maybe the doctor had done something evil. And possibly he would be asked to pay the additional hospital bill out of his own pocket.

So, the PSRO conditions being met, she went home. And climbing the stairs two days later, she suffered a fatal heart attack. Looking back over that last day in the hospital, the consultant for the plaintiff's lawyers points out that maybe there was a little evidence of electrical instability in that ECG and that her medications and electrolyte values should be rechecked because of the danger of an arrhythmia.

Such a case tells us of the glaring faults and shortcomings of the PSRO as now being advocated by federal and local government. In addition, it may signal one of the most famous law suits in the history of American medicine. The chairman of the local PSRO could, of course, be sued for malpractice. It was his insistence on meeting these arbitrary rules that forced the patient to be sent home before the doctor felt it was wise. This caused her death.

Such painful examples can be strung out far longer than this editorial should stretch. They merely emphasize that the definition of the length of stay, permissible charges, and norms for patient care (instituted by a self-appointed peerage) may constitute peer review; they do not constitute either the practice of medicine or the definition of high quality care. . . .

Peering dimly into the future, then, we can discern what sorts of peers will do the peer review. We predict that they will constitute a new nobility (authority without peer), peering into the records of patients written by physicians whom they no longer regard as their peers. An essentially malignant process, this cancer will be lethal and PSRO will die. . . .

Dr. Moore is, of course, far from alone among physicians in having great fears about the workability and justice of the PSRO legislation. Nor are physicians alone in their fears. From the side of professional consumer representatives, for example, Professor Sylvia A. Law of New

York University has recently suggested that, with regard to PSRO, "the patient may, however, have been lost in the shuffle." She fears that under PSRO, patients may be deprived of medical and related care to which they are entitled. She notes that "in a fee for service system the physican has a financial incentive to serve as the patient's advocate in obtaining the care prescribed." But, she adds, "if, as in a health maintenance organization, the financial incentive is reversed, the physician may be less likely to go through the processes needed to obtain authorization for care that produces no financial benefit."

To solve the dilemma, Professor Law suggests:

> . . . a whole new class of health service worker is needed to work in close conjunction with physicians and individuals to make information accessible to patients, to know and explain alternatives, and to represent individuals to make information accessible to patients, to know and explain alternatives, and to represent individuals in the decision-making process.[13]

But if PSRO's effect is to add a whole new class of health workers to the already swollen health-care work force, its effectiveness as a cost-cutting device—the main reason Congress passed this legislation—is likely to be still further impaired.

CONCLUSION

The reflections on PSRO above have been gloomy. This writer obviously has grave reservations about PSRO and its effect upon American medical care, particularly upon important ancillary matters such as the confidentiality of the patient-physician relationship. Nevertheless, PSRO is the law of the land, and it is going to be implemented. One must hope that with experience both the advantages and the disadvantages of PSRO will become more clear, and that Congress will act in timely fashion to maximize the advantages and minimize or end the disadvantages.

NOTES

1. *Medical Care Expenditures, Prices, and Costs: Background Book* (Washington, D.C.: Department of Health, Education, and Welfare Publication No. [SSA] 74-11909, September 1973), p. 9.
2. Harry Schwartz, *The Case for American Medicine* (New York: David McKay, 1972), p. 130.
3. American Medical Association Board of Trustees, *Analysis and Implementation of AMA Policy on PSRO Adopted by House of Delegates, Anaheim, California*, p. 1 (mimeographed paper distributed January 24, 1974, at AMA Leadership Conference in Chicago).
4. *Ibid.*, p. 2.
5. Letter to the Editor, *American Journal of Public Health* (October 1974), p. 1007.
6. This discussion is based upon material in the *Bulletin of the American College of Surgeons* (March 1974), p. 11.
7. Ian R. Lawson, "Professional Standards Review Organization and Care of the Elderly," *Journal of the American Medical Association* (July 15, 1974), pp. 312–313.
8. *American Journal of Public Health, op. cit.*
9. *New York Times,* September 30, October 1 and 2, 1974.
10. *New York Times,* June 24, 1974.
11. *The Wall Street Journal,* October 7, 1974.
12. Francis D. Moore, "Peer Review and All That," *Archives of Surgery* (April 1974), pp. 397–398.
13. Sylvia A. Law, *Blue Cross: What Went Wrong?* (New Haven, Conn.: Yale University Press, 1974), pp. 142–144.

EIGHT

Portfolio Decisions
and Social Responsibility

Roger G. Kennedy

Vice-President, Ford Foundation

One day I was having a Wall Street lunch, and present in the crowd was a pulp-and-paper magnate. He announced to the table that the energy crisis and the recession had so scattered "the environmentalists and proxy fighters" that management was again free to disregard any other stockholder interest than the price of the stock. Was he right? Was "investor social responsibility" just a luxury of the bull market? I don't think so.

The facts don't sustain his declaration. Despite recession and falling stock prices in 1974, investors were enough interested in the conduct of corporate management as it affected society (not just how it affected the bottom line) to triple the number of issues which received the required percentage of the proxy support to stay on the ballots for next year. Something new has entered in American corporate life, something which has had many explanations and awaits a coherent theory. But though new in practice, it does seem to grow out of one of the oldest ideas in our tradition, the idea of a social compact.

Investors are acting as if they believed that to possess assets at all is to take on responsibility to sustain that fragile artifact, society, an artifact

- in which love and joy, beauty and creative work are given some shelter and scope;
- in which greed, lust, hate, envy, and the urge to destroy are channelled by law and custom;
- in which neither any ego nor the community is permitted to overwhelm the other; and
- which provides for mutual defense, sharing of burdens, some choice of tasks and scope for public ambition.

Investors are behaving as if they believed that within society certain specialized organizations are permitted to exist so long as they perform their assigned tasks and live by the rules. These include chartered corporations and foundations, colleges (from a Roman word for a limited corporation), universities (from the Roman word for an all-purpose corporation), churches, mutual funds, labor unions, municipalities, trustees, partnerships, civil marriages, and cemetery associations.

To receive society's protection, these institutions must be useful. Some, like foundations, are given charters which come right out and tell us their social purposes. Others, like most profit-seeking corporations, are given charters which are silent about their social purposes.

None of them would exist but for a civil order, and they are all governed by men who can be expected to behave morally. These similarities overwhelm their apparent differences of function.

FUNCTIONS OF INVESTMENT MANAGERS

That is not to say that there are no differences in stated functions. The first social responsibility of an investment manager is to serve the chartered purposes of the institution whose assets are given into his trust. For example, a university investment officer's first task is to assure the continuity of the context for the criticism and sustenance of ideas. That context includes faculty and buildings; books; blackboards, especially erasers; ivy on Old Main; and lemon, cream, and sugar at the Faculty Club.

The pension fund manager enters into a covenant to maintain as best he can the purchasing power of savings put into his care lest his subscribers be left untended in their age and infirmity. Specialized endowments for libraries and museums, orchestras, churches and theaters, hospitals and addiction centers—all must be managed first to keep these organisms functioning.

The first social consideration of the investment process of these funds is survival. That is enough, and more than enough, to ask of the baffled men who worry about the financial fortunes. Yet we do ask more.

Especially do we ask more of the financial management of institutions which exist only to serve others, which have no primary duty to perpetuate themselves, bricks, staff, grass, or faculty. Many foundations, for example, are chartered to serve the public welfare, but they break down into several categories, which in turn determine how they use their assets to serve the public.

THE NATURE OF FOUNDATIONS

For example, some foundations are *assertive* and some are *reactive*. Some set out to achieve social goals, like equalizing access to education or opportunity in employment, seeking justice under the law, or finding new strains of rice or corn. These goals are not likely to be achieved unless assertive philanthropy goes out and finds people to go after them. An assertive philanthropy, as an investor, acts quite differently from, say, a reactive philanthropy, and very differently from a single-purpose endowment. The practical consequences of an assertive role is to adopt what might be called a "total resources" doctrine.

By "survival" I meant sustaining funds to support philanthropic programs. Long ago several boards of trustees of foundations eliminated any artificial barrier between the use of income, or even of total return (which includes capital gains when they had any) and the use of principal. They decided to try to survive and, at the same time, to apply their total resources to their social purposes. This meant spending larger amounts of capital than portfolio policy, operating alone, could have justified. It has also meant making program-related investments, accepting more risk and less return than the market might provide. This total resources doctrine is only available to an institution which is not committed to a physical plant—campus or library, bricks or stone—and which is free to alter its priorities and its objectives as society alters. A total resources doctrine can be an invitation to profligacy; it requires stern self-discipline. It has some, but not many, adherents.

THE INTEGRITY DOCTRINE

There is a more limited view of the relationship of the portfolio to social policy which has broader appeal. It could be called the Integrity Doctrine. It holds that the right hand should know what the left is doing. If a church is preaching against alcohol, it should not own distilleries. If a foundation supports research and information to inform the public of the peril of smoking, it should not draw income from the sale of cigarettes. For many years the College Retirement Equities Fund has refrained from owning either liquor or tobacco stocks under its "butts and booze" doctrine.

The Integrity Doctrine is much more difficult to apply, of course, when a corporation engages in one activity which seems incompatible with the social objectives of an endowed institution and at the same time in another activity which advances another such objective. A big polluter may also be an outstanding hirer of minorities. A corrupter of venal politicians may leave the air and water uncorrupted. These conflicting considerations require discrimination, but the fact is that they are no more subtle than many other offsetting balances in the investment process. The investor seeking integrity has a complex job, not a simple one.

THE AVOIDANCE OF SOCIAL INJURY DOCTRINE

The least strenuous mode of applying social considerations to the investment process is what the Yale investment committee calls "the avoidance of social injury." This position requires that the investor not drink from a polluted income stream. It requires him not to make his capital available to an enterprise which injures his social values. For most educational institutions these values would include, for example, redressing the effects of centuries of racial and sex discrimination.

The last principle (explained at length in *The Ethical Investor* by Jon Gunneman, Charles Powers, and John Simon, Yale University Press, 1972) provides a basis for portfolio decisions in those very rare cases in which the investor knows that the investment of his funds will make it easier for a corporation to do a social injury. The authors make it plain that they don't think this will happen often. Social injury is seldom both obvious and legal. The investor doesn't often detect it before regulators or legislators, but the avoider of social injury would be bound to abstain from profiting from it at society's expense.

The set of objectives of the adherent to the integrity doctrine, on the other hand, may not be fixed in legislation or even in the opinions of the majority, but his portfolio policy would be determined by a requirement that what he does with his investment dollars not conflict with what he does with the dollar benefits of investment.

This may seem very theoretical, and far removed from the cockpit of investment decision. It is. Personally, I find the sort of "theological" discussion which I have just reviewed distracts more than it aids the daily difficulty of trying to live a moral life while living as an investor. I find it more helpful to distinguish between the corporation, which is a thing, and managers, employees, stockholders, customers, and neighbors, who are persons. The business corporation is a powerful agent of social change. It was brought into being in order to attract capital to certain activities which society, acting initially through the Crown and later through legislatures, thought useful. It is not an organic growth of nature. It exists not of its own right, but to be used.

STOCKHOLDER ACTIONS

Those who commenced stockholder actions in recent years treated the business corporation in this way. As moral persons they sought to direct the huge but morally neutral power of the business corporation to achieve specific moral purposes.

The first such purpose was local: Saul Alinsky's effort to make Kodak into an agent to end racial discrimination in Rochester, New York, in 1966. FIGHT had limited objectives. It wanted more black people hired in one upstate New York city. Project GM, which came along next, was national. It wanted to impel General Motors into action to enhance minority employment opportunities and at the same time change the way General Motors governed itself. Project GM, though limited to one company and to one country, tried to do two things at once, and hence confused for many people efforts to change corporate behavior with efforts to change corporate governance.

Project GM scored a partial success. One can argue about the links in the chain of cause and effect, but GM did alter the composition of its board to make it broader. Thereafter a lot of other corporations included blacks and women and more people with experience in worrying about consumers rather than producers.

Next came the effort to use Honeywell proxy statements to alter American foreign policy, specifically in Southeast Asia. Though their attack was upon weapons production generally, Charles Pillsbury and his friends who sought as stockholders to persuade Honeywell not to produce weapons ordered by the Department of Defense would not have been very likely to have used the proxy device to deny corporate production of military goods directed at Japanese after Pearl Harbor or to defeat the Luftwaffe. The Honeywell project had little hope of altering corporate action: it used the annual meeting as a forum to debate foreign policy.

Later proxy actions also sought to draw attention to the presence of a flow of income to Portuguese colonialists and to South Africans enforcing apartheid, and attention to the absence in many countries in Asia and Latin America of effective food and drug regulation.

The advocates of these proxy actions believed that corporate action might be expected to change a little and, as a result, that some governmental action or the conditions of life in some foreign countries might improve a little. That was, and is, enough to justify all the exertion of activist groups and the use of the proxy device.

The portfolio manager, observing this, can join in the effort initiated by others in the form of proxy actions, but it is important to stress that he does not have to wait for somebody else. Nor are his means of behaving responsibly limited to voting proxies. Let's say it again: The corporation is morally neutral, as indifferent to conscience as a railroad engine, a hippopotamus, or a giant squid. But people in corporations are as moral and susceptible to suggestion as those paragons of invidious virtue, philanthropists, professors, or journalists. How does one man get the attention of another? How do you encourage him in the good fight? How do you listen to him? For they and you and I—managers, employees, neighbors of the plant, consumers of products—are all intertwined with the stockholder or bondholder in a network of responsibility which comes out of the social contract.

As Project GM demonstrated, the morally neutral bulk of a giant corporation can be nudged by clamor—mere clamor. Argument, publicity, stockholder suits, or proxy proposals all bring above the noise level certain matters crying to be heard and given attention. As Theodore Roosevelt might have said, a stockholder's annual meeting is a bully platform. There are more people at proxy meetings than in many churches or lecture halls. More people read proxy statements than books on corporate responsibility.

After clamor comes litigation as a method; an example would be the current suit by certain stockholders against the management of Northrup Aviation to recover corporate funds spent for campaign contributions. This lawsuit moves in concert with stockholder resolutions on proxy statements.

Proxy proposals are old hat by now, but it is worth noting just how successful they were in this bear market, recession year. Nearly thirty stockholder resolutions got enough stockholder support to get reconsideration next year, an astonishing achievement, three times the number in 1973.

After proxy actions comes letterwriting, sometimes a more effective tool than a mere marking of a ballot. Well-reasoned letters which don't assume the writer to be more moral than the reader often get attention and even provoke positive action. Active dialogue with management, eye-to-eye breaking bread together also can affect behavior along the margin. That is, after all, what the concerned investor is after: making some improvement in the behavior of people—not merely feeling good.

Finally, research into specific subjects, such as energy policy or the ways in which brand-name drugs are marketed internationally, can produce information which in the hands of corporate management or legislatures, can afford behavior for the better. The ethical investor may become so interested in a subject that he wants to know more than he learned in a proxy fight, and he may want to help others learn about the subject, too.

As you have by now observed, nothing good has been said here for the lovely idea that portfolio policy can meet its social responsibility by owning good companies and not owning bad ones. This is a beguiling thought until you try to define what you mean by good and bad, and until the mingled goodness and badness in corporate action—like human action—becomes obvious. But "white lists" or "black lists" are appealing to people who think corporate officers are one class of moral beings and they, the corporate critics, are of another, high order.

The job is harder than a one-time buy-or-sell decision. It is certainly harder than an aye or nay vote of confidence, once and for all, in corporate management for everything or nothing they do, without discrimination.

CONCLUSION

What is required, it seems to me, is that those human beings who happen to be portfolio managers should deal with those human beings who happen to be corporate managers with some recognition that we are all stumbling down an ill-lighted trail, from quandary to quandary, uncertain, unwise, doing the best we can to live as morally as we are able. All of us are tied together by mutual benefits and mutual obligations. Each of us seeks to make small adjustments in the way the social compact functions as the world changes, to strike new balances of justice among those affected by that immensely powerful but ethically neutral agent—the business corporation. Consumers, employees, the community, stockholders, bondholders, management—all have interlocking objectives. It is not true that what one gains must be at the expense of all the others. None would gain if the fragile structure which permits them all the benefit, the society which allows the corporation to exist, were to be rent apart. It is in that light, I think, that social considerations must be applied to portfolio decisions.

NINE

A Guide to
Social Responsibility of
the Multinational Enterprise

Ingo Walter

Professor, Economics and Finance
New York University

Most people today believe that economic interdependence among the world's nations brings with it political, social, and material benefits that, on balance, far outweigh the transitional economic disturbances and dislocations which are part of the process of change. The international economic order that has evolved during the past several decades is now committed to substantial and growing freedom in the exchange of goods and services, factors of production, and ideas—both regionally and globally.[1] Whether for good or ill, multinational enterprise has emerged as the one form of economic organization that seems best able to survive and prosper in an interdependent world of sovereign national states and to adapt quickly and efficiently to intercountry variations in resource availability, productive efficiency, and useful knowledge.

Motivated in part by long-term profit and corporate survival, the firm operates with minimal effective regard for political frontiers, reconciling national and international competitive disequilibria, raising levels of real income, and widening the range of product choice. At its best, the multinational corporation can serve as a catalyst in the international economy, accelerating the process of adjustment to new and more rational production patterns in response to changing economic and technological conditions, and generating benefits that are widely and equitably diffused. At its worst, its economic power can transcend that of duly constituted governmental authority and enable it to obstruct if not negate choices made by sovereign states through political processes.

There has been much discussion in recent years about the role of multinational enterprise in global and national political and economic affairs. More often than not, the debate has been staged against a highly charged backdrop of confrontation between protagonists identified with differing ideological positions, relying on biased or questionable evidence.[2] This essay considers some of the principal sources of friction between the multinational enterprise and national interests within the framework of corporate social responsibility. The issue is discussed from the standpoint of conflicting objectives and patterns of behavior. Its focus is on defining a common ground—on the reconciliation of differences through considered weighing of fundamental costs and benefits associated with alternative corporate and public policy decisions.

We begin by reviewing briefly the nature of the multinational enterprise: What it is, what it does, how it behaves, and how to measure its impact on society when there are deep divisions of opinion on the appropriate yardsticks for measurement as well as the evaluation of performance itself. We next turn to the definition of corporate social responsibility in a multinational context, and propose a set of practical guidelines that can be used by management to help sort out the issues and provide the basis for a coherent set of corporate policies. We then survey rather systematically the principal sources of conflict between the multinational firm and its environment and, in accordance with the guidelines we have developed, suggest policy responses that are both internally and externally consistent and capable of implementation.

As we proceed, we are forced to make some judgment, on the basis of available evidence, of multinational corporate performance in each of the relevant conflict zones. The results rather decisively refute the thesis of inherent and permanent antagonism and polarization of interest between the multinational firm and the nation-state. Instead, the two are partners in a nonzero-sum game in which both can gain in a mutually advantageous working relationship. Periodic conflict is inevitable, just as it is between business and society at the national level. It is often acerbic and politically visible. But conciliation is usually both possible and fundamentally in the interest of both sides.

MOTIVATION AND IMPACT ASSESSMENT

It is perhaps best to start a discussion of social responsibility by avoiding normative issues altogether, to concentrate entirely on *how multinational firms operate*—what makes them tick, how they react to external events, and how they can influence national economies. The intent is to identify the important sources of social gain and social conflict, and to raise at the very start the problem of overall impact evaluation as a setting for the policy-oriented discussion that follows.

Varied Motivation

Like national enterprise, management of multinational firms must focus rather consistently on providing an adequate return on invested capital. Long-range profit-maximizing behavior in a multinational setting—to the extent that it is indeed followed by the firm—takes on at least seven more or less distinct dimensions, most of them positive but some negative from the standpoint of national and international welfare. It is the latter that give rise to conflict between the firm and the nation.

First is the creation of *information efficiency* applied to the use of available resources at each production site and to optimal resource use within a global logistical network. This involves intrafirm transfers of managerial and technical knowhow, as well as the collection and interpretation of information on markets, raw materials, and other inputs. It also involves reduced reaction time on the part of the firm to shifts in supply and demand factors. Imperfect information and slow adjustment long have been two of the principal barriers to effective competition and efficiency in the international economy; minimization of both represents an important contribution of the multinational enterprise and a major source of its competitive advantage.[3]

Second, efficiency in *resource allocation* is achieved by shifting, at the margin, the location of production to reduce input costs of relatively immobile factors—such as land, labor, and natural resources—and to improve the productive use of relatively mobile factors, particularly capital. Input combinations are rearranged as a result of multinational business operations, both within and between types of resources. The multinational enterprise thus promotes specialization and trade in the international economy according to the dictates of comparative advantage. It accelerates and magnifies the traditional gains from the rational allocation of international production.[4]

Third, there are efficiencies made possible by *economies of scale* at individual plants wholly or partly specialized in assembly operations or in production of components and parts—and other partial production processes—and through scale economies achieved in management service functions as well as product- and process-related research and development activities. By applying a consistent set of performance criteria within the firm's production, distribution, and administrative planning system, it can maintain pressure at the operations level to exploit fully opportunities for scale-related efficiencies wherever they develop.

A fourth behavioral characteristic is reduction, where possible, of *uncertainties* associated with operating in multiple national business environments involving political, economic, and financial risks that do not exist in purely national operations. Increased risk requires a commensurately higher rate of return on invested capital, and at the same time generates dual pressures for international diversification and uncertainty-reducing adjustments in the national regulatory environment. Hedging foreign-exchange risk and minimizing equity exposure in politically unstable countries are two examples. Risk reduction may involve abrupt shifts in company policy, which in turn may have destabilizing effects on important financial and economic variables.[5]

A fifth dimension is the use of increased *product-market control* which may reduce the level of effective competition and raise prices above full cost or compromise product quality. Pressures to reduce competition and monopolize markets seem to be endemic in almost all forms of economic organization, and the multinational enterprise—operating from a strong competitive base—may cause increased concentration particularly in small markets characterized by comparatively weak indigenous firms.

A sixth element is the possibility of increased *factor-market control.* Particularly in developing countries where the multinational firm is a major employer of resources (especially labor), its position may under certain conditions be used to exert downward pressure on prices. Off-shore manufacturing for reexport may occasionally be susceptible to monopsonistic behavior in local markets for productive inputs.

A final motivational element is to *avoid governmental obstacles* to efficient operation and maximum financial return. For example, shifts in production and distribution patterns can be used to circumvent tariffs and other barriers to market access, and restrictions on sources of raw-materials supplies. Financing practices may be modified to side-step barriers to international capital mobility, and more generally to minimize the firm's tax burden and avoid controls on international payments.

This simple listing of some of the basic characteristics of multinational corporate behavior implies strongly that its impact on society at the national level must constitute a complex mixture of positive and negative elements to identify, assess, weigh, and set off against an equally complex matrix of national constraints and objectives.

Varied Operating Characteristics

Within a given country the multinational firm may maintain extractive or production facilities, wholly owned or in joint venture, supplying goods or services to the domestic market, for export to the firm's home country, or for export to third countries. Operations may range from assembly of imported components and parts for domestic sale or reexport to partial or complete manufacture from materials procured locally. The firm may also operate distribution and service facilities in the local market and (less commonly) engage in research and development. From the home country's point of view, the firm may produce abroad goods that were formerly exported, open up new markets, or supply the domestic market from an overseas "export platform"—each of which may in turn involve new exports of raw materials, intermediate goods, capital equipment, or knowhow.

The multinational's initial investment in a given affiliate may be undertaken *de novo,* or it may involve partial or complete acquisition of preexisting facilities owned locally or by third-country nationals. Initial and recurring financial needs may be met through retained earnings of the affiliate, further infusions of equity or loans from the parent firm, equity participation and borrowings in the indigenous capital market, or loans and equity from local government sources. Manpower requirements, after an initial start-up phase, are normally satisfied from the local labor force, with skill needs met partly by drawing workers away from existing firms, partly from new graduates of the educational- and technical-training establishments, and partly through in-company training programs. Top and middle management in line and staff positions at first tend to be foreign nationals from the parent firm or third-country affiliates, but within a relatively short period of time expatriate involvement typically recedes. Major policy decisions tend to be made at corporate headquarters or at regional management centers, and the firm may be organized along geographic or product lines—or some form of "matrix" organization may be attempted.[6]

The multinational enterprise thus infuses part of its financial and human-resource needs from abroad, and mobilizes the remainder within the host economy. It also contributes production technology, in the abstract and embodied in imported capital equipment, which may or may not be readily adapted to local conditions. Management and marketing knowhow—particularly in product development and design; quality control; production scheduling; organizational design;

planning; and budgeting, merchandising, and finance, together with employee motivation and development—are equally significant inputs. And continued access to markets and material supplies abroad, as well as permanent access to technical and managerial advances developed abroad, are typically important and continuing aspects of multinational corporate involvement in national economies.

Measuring the Impacts

Because of the varied motivational and operating characteristics of multinational firms, *ex ante* evaluation of their reaction to external influences is bound to be superficial and perhaps foolhardy. In part, this is because each firm has an unique profile comprising organization structure, management competence, interpersonal relations, historical development, philosophy or value system, goals and strategies, product and geographic coverage, relationships with home and host country governments, and the like. Each reflects in its behavior, elements of its home culture: American, Swiss, Japanese, British, German, French, and so on. Each has a different "options matrix" which determines what it can do under different circumstances and how it will react to changes in its environment. Nor do multinationals (like national companies) necessarily optimize or plan continuously, which seriously impedes behavioral forecasting. No firm behaves exactly like any other, and this erodes the credibility of all homogeneous solutions to problems associated with multinational corporate operations.[7]

Equally problematic is *ex post* assessment of their impact on national social and economic life. Countries are interested in the balance-of-payments implications of capital inflows, earnings remissions, and the like. They are interested in the trade effects of foreign direct investment, in terms of imports displaced and exports generated (or exports displaced and imports generated). They are interested in new income and employment created, taxes paid, labor trained, technology transferred, prices charged, and a host of other issues. They are also interested in operational stability and the risk of abrupt disengagement if conditions change. And they are interested in the broader effects on societal development. The classic question is: What would things have looked like if multinational corporate involvement had been foregone? Until an "alternative" assessment has been made, very little can be said. And because the alternative vector hinges on *assumptions,* impact assessment of multinational corporations depends fundamentally on the particular hypothetical alternatives posited by the investigator.[8]

Even if a plausible and objective impact assessment can be developed, it remains difficult to strike a balance for policy purposes unless the results can be reconciled with the collective preferences of the host country—what economists call the "objective function"— really a selection or coalescence from a diverse pool of individual and group preferences that is inherently unstable. Because it is politically determined, the objective function may differ markedly over time and among countries. Some societal goals may be both stable and consistent: minimum unemployment; maximum level and growth of real income per capita; price-level stability; improved nutrition, health, and education are examples. Others differ widely from one country to the next: regional balance in economic development, income leveling, the desirability of democratic institutions, and the treatment of racial and ethnic minorities are some examples. Still others may shift significantly over time; for example, the value placed on domestic ownership of the means of production, economic independence, consumer protection, environmental damage, and perceived vulnerability to "foreign" cultural and political influences. Precisely the same pattern of multinational corporate behavior considered entirely legitimate in a particular country today may be deemed socially irresponsible in a neighboring country, or in the same country a few years hence. Such two-dimensional variance in societal goals means that evaluation of the performance of multinational enterprise can be legitimately carried out only with specific reference to time and place.

To further compound the problem, objective and balanced assessment of economic and social costs and benefits of multinational corporate operations aligned with accurately perceived local objectives and preferences still may not yield consistent and unambigous policy prescriptions. National decision systems differ, encompassing complex and changing interrelationships among political parties; special-interest groups; the media; the military; and the various executive, legislative, and judicial organs of government. There may also be significant differences between national and subnational objectives, and in the acceptability of illegal and quasi-legal dealings such as bribery and black market transactions. And does government really speak for the people, or does it primarily reflect elite attitudes with the result that its policies toward multinational firms may actually exacerbate existing inequities at the national level? The upshot is that managers tend to be understandably unsure of themselves when it comes to defining socially responsible company policies. The rules of the game differ and change, the signals are contradictory, information is incomplete, and sometimes the characteristic of multinationality itself is at the base of conflict, as we shall see.

CORPORATE SOCIAL RESPONSIBILITY IN A MULTINATIONAL SETTING

A great deal has been written about corporate social responsibility, much of which seems to conclude that a fundamental restructuring at the national level of the relationship between the firm and society is presently underway. The prevailing view appears to be that the firm must periodically follow lines of action that in some measure help society attain one or more of its goals, as determined by the political process. Such policies, even if not immediately profitable, are presumed ultimately to redound to the benefit of the enterprise and its shareholders.[9] The opposing view, that "the business of business is business" and that it is socially undesirable (indeed dangerous) to vest managers with the power to define and pursue specific social values without political mandate or accountability, has in recent years lost ground in most countries.[10] Certainly with the existence of powerful public institutions business cannot with impunity behave at variance with prevailing social objectives for very long. On the other hand, there also seem to be limits, however ill-defined, beyond which business voluntarism makes little sense.[11]

The Issue of Social Responsibility

The pressures come from many sides. Consumers want better and safer products, advertised, labeled, packaged, sold, financed and serviced honestly, with ample disclosure for comparison purposes. The days of *caveat emptor* are dying, and producer liability has grown apace—in some sectors "negative proof" is taking hold, with products having to be proven acceptable *before* they can be marketed, rather than proven unacceptable afterward. And the new rules of the game in market behavior are gradually advancing even as the old rules of effective price and quality competition are being ever more strictly enforced. In addition, there are persistent, often inconsistent and conflicting demands that business reduce its despoilation of the natural environment (both directly and through its products), contribute to the resolution of urban, racial, and other social ills, provide bountiful philanthropy, and generally align its operations with government policies and the "popular opinion" of the times.

Within the firm itself, employees are demanding better conditions of work, including increased attention to health, safety, noise, pensions, and the like—but also extending to industrial democracy and an expanded worker role in management decisions. Personal self-esteem may be more fundamental for many employees than a democratic "voice" in management decisions, however. And many workers work not to obtain direct satisfaction or a sense of accomplishment, but rather to obtain the means to pursue nonwork objectives. Meanwhile, shareholders continue to press for a greater voice in running the companies they own (or at least finding out a little more about it), particularly insofar as business policy relates to the major social issues of the day.[12]

Reacting to social pressures is no easy task. Frequently, the most influential critics are self-appointed spokesmen for particular groups or causes who use the media and the courts with great skill. Quite unlike business, very little social control appears to be exercised over the "activist-media-legal" complex, and accountability to the public on the part of those involved is minimal. It is certainly not clear to what extent social pressures on business reflect grass-roots sentiment, and to what extent they reflect the views of individuals and groups who think they discern such sentiment.

Even governmental control of business, nominally under a clear public mandate, takes on a bureaucratic dynamic of its own, often characterized by gross inconsistency, excessive zeal, susceptibility to error, and a peculiarly static, textbook view of normative competitive relationships. There is the diversity of sources of governmental action, alongside the bureaucratic stance of single sources, that needs to be confronted as well. Mistakes are made and quickly forgotten. Coherent planning is dissipated. Projects eventually proven socially desirable are delayed for extended periods with no accounting for the interim benefits foregone. Business risks rise, and so does the cost of information and defensive activities. Clearly, the kind of reasoned socioeconomic cost-benefit analysis needed is characteristic neither of the business sector nor of its critics and regulators, and social control perhaps inevitably ends up as a messy, slow, costly, and confrontational iteration.[13]

Management has been slow to respond to the redefinition of its role in society. The old corporate arrogance is largely gone, at least publicly, and to some extent so is the early reliance on extensive public relations efforts backed by little or no substance. Firms are moving ahead (some rapidly and some sluggishly) on environmental safeguards, employment opportunities, working conditions, and consumer protection—although the extent to which competition allows costly voluntary acts is arguable. A recent survey of annual reports of 600 major U.S. corporations shows a marked increase in explicit statements of social concerns and actions at the company level from 167 in 1965 to 576 in 1971, and a qualitative shift from philanthropic and community-oriented aspects to environmental and consumer-related issues.[14]

Both the trend and the qualitative shift in social concerns have been corroborated in two independent studies, one covering personal commitments of a sample of top American executives, the other surveying a very large group of U.S. corporate managers.[15] There is, of course, a good deal of slippage between what people say, what they think, and how they actually perform. In a few firms, the role of the chief executive and the way it is carried out is itself undergoing change, and "business statesmen" are gradually beginning to emerge, concerned both with social responsibility and with its limits—and able to present their arguments cogently and eloquently.

Still, much of traditional business narrowness and inarticulateness remains, and inhibits effective debate on the issues. Management itself often seems of two minds. One businessman in a candid moment has observed, "When a business statesman makes public speeches, he has to talk in terms of social responsibility and long-term profit maximization, but the truth—the deep secret he can never admit to anyone except the lady who shares his pillow—is that he is a short-term profit maximizer." [16] And the critics remain largely unimpressed—a recent broad-based survey of American social activists found 43 percent highly antagonistic toward business' overall performance in society, as against 29 percent who were generally supportive of business behavior. [17] Social responsibility, as an issue that must be addressed by management in all of its complex and changing dimensions, is here to stay.

The Multinational Scene

Sizable as the problem of social responsibility may be in a general sense, the issue confronting the enterprise in a multinational business environment is far more complex—it is forced to confront a host of social issues *in addition to* those it must face in the national environment, and the penalties for failure may be much more severe. The firm operates in multiple social, political, and economic settings, each with a different historical pattern of development, set of current conditions, and collectively determined national goal structure. Not only do the aforementioned problems of aligning business policy with prevailing social objectives confront the firm in a different way in each national setting, making more difficult or even precluding a consistent set of company policies, but acceptable business behavior in any one country may also run counter to public policy or group interests elsewhere. Moreover, it almost always faces an inherent dual standard in host countries, with social conflicts involving multinational firms viewed more seriously than the same kinds of conflicts involving indigenous enterprises. And, if the responsibilities of a firm to society are viewed as having to be commensurate with its power (its size and its potential influence on its environment), then surely multinational firms are especially susceptible to pressures from this quarter and must conduct themselves accordingly—even if these pressures are often fragmented and at cross-purposes.

The multinational enterprise can attempt to approach this dilemma in three ways. It can adopt a predominantly *passive* attitude, considering itself the object of social controls imposed by each of the nations in which it operates, to which it aligns its operations in such a way as to safeguard its own interests while above all minimizing friction. It can adopt a *pro-active* position, whereby the firm recognizes the critical importance of the social controls imposed upon it but at the same time attempts to "manage" or influence the regulatory and attitudinal environment. Or it can assume an *adaptive* posture, imposing upon itself voluntarily patterns of behavior that are continuously sensitive to prevailing social issues.[18]

From the standpoint of the multinational firm the *passive* alternative is generally unacceptable and counterproductive, indeed socially irresponsible as a viable strategy. If society's goals and policies are set in an interactive way through the political process, then the firm has an obligation to participate and to defend its interests as best it can within accepted limits of conduct. Only when the issue involves the very character of the multinational enterprise as an institution, or fundamental questions of national destiny wherein the firm's role is trivial, can a passive "low profile" be justified.

Consider instead the *pro-active* alternative.[19] Most multinationals originate in highly advanced societies such as the United States. Attempts to restrict competition have been met with antitrust legislation. Attempts to exploit the market brought forth a host of regulatory agencies, including (in the United States) the Food and Drug Administration, the Federal Trade Commission, the Federal Power Commission, the Interstate Commerce Commission, and the like. Whatever slack remained has in recent years been taken up by the emergence of strong consumer advocacy groups. Attempts to exploit productive-factor markets and environmental resources have been met with the creation of the Securities and Exchange Commission, the National Labor Relations Board, the Environmental Protection Agency, as well as strong labor unions and a host of pressure groups with a variety of causes ranging from pollution control to migrant workers to shareholder rights.

The point is that the multinationals' home countries have created, over time, a "web of social control" which, though not always efficient, serves as a constraint on those motivations of the enterprise that are actually or potentially in conflict with prevailing social objectives. The pro-active enterprise, meanwhile, does what it can to influence the social-control web that surrounds it. The counterbalancing forces create a dynamic equilibrium, with constant pressure and counter-pressure. There are periodic excesses on both sides, and considerable information and transactions costs fall on business, consumer, and taxpayer alike.[20] It is an equilibrium, nevertheless, and departures from its politically determined constraints are soon rectified.

When the pro-active firm goes abroad, it typically faces a set of social controls quite different from those existing at home, sometimes stronger but often far weaker. The firm's behavior pattern, fundamentally conditioned by the home environment even after lengthy experience abroad, under the pro-active hypothesis remains much the same. It probes the strengths and weaknesses of the surrounding tissue of social controls in each host country in order to obtain and maintain conditions of entry, operations, and earnings remission as closely aligned as possible to company objectives. If the web of social controls is undeveloped, or in the early stages of development, the firm may adopt policies or engage in individual actions that may ultimately be considered socially irresponsible. The situation may continue for some time while countervailing forces gather strength, and is likely to result in a subsequent clash that will harm both sides but should surprise neither. The incidence of such cases, this view would predict, will be higher in less developed than in developed countries, higher in countries with market-oriented economies than in economies with substantial elements of central planning and control, and higher in democracies than in totalitarian states. This generalization will not of course hold up well under unstable conditions, as when a government is overthrown—regardless of the nature of the successor—and the multinational firm is identified with the policies of the defunct regime.

The pro-active hypothesis presupposes that the multinational firm will not in fact impose *upon itself* (or adapt to host-country conditions) the kinds of behavioral constraints that are imposed upon it in its home environment or in third countries. It simply plays by the rules—no more and no less—and it tries to influence those rules. It is fundamentally up to each nation to establish the regulatory framework that will minimize the net social costs of multinational corporate involvement without at the same time sacrificing the associated economic benefits. This is not easy. The multinational firm often has available to it an extraordinarily wide range of alternatives which permit it to "opt out" of (or abstain from) a hostile environment, and host nations must determine a threshold level of regulation and control that may not be exceeded without sacrificing benefits which the multinational firm provides and which cannot be obtained elsewhere at comparable cost. On balance, consistently pro-active behavior of this sort is hardly optimal. It is confrontational, costly, and crisis prone. In some industries, such as pharmaceuticals, it is almost unthinkable.

Consider now the *adaptive* alternative. When it seems appropriate in the light of evident societal objectives the firm is willing to do *more* than it is forced to do by the regulatory environment. From what has already been said about intercountry variations in that environment, a uniform set of global policies targeted on social issues seems out of the question. And, to the extent such policies entail costs, they may indeed be precluded by competitive factors. The real problem facing management of the adaptive multinational company is to decide what policies to apply under very specific areas of real or potential conflict. Neither consistently pro-active, passive, nor voluntary behavior makes sense under all conditions in all countries. What multinational business needs is a way to devise an optimal response pattern for social issues—one that safeguards the firm's own interests while minimizing the chance of conflict and competitive dislocations.

To accomplish this, it seems reasonable to draw flexibly on the three basic behavior patterns identified here, and to match them against the various sources of conflict encountered by the multinational firm in a kind of matrix format. The intent is to define which sources of conflict fall into each normative behavior profile, and to assign appropriate company policies to deal with them. Three distinct, though not mutually exclusive, forms of behavior stand out as appropriate under conflict conditions regularly encountered by the multinational enterprise: (1) *Compliance-oriented behavior,* involving strict adherence to constraints imposed by duly constituted public authority, but not precluding an advocacy role, requiring imposition of few additional behavioral guidelines by the firm on itself; (2) *Selective voluntarism,* requiring the development of a baseline corporate policy targeted on specific social responsibility issues that can be modified efficiently to meet often poorly defined local conditions; and (3) *Avoidance-oriented behavior,* involving conflict inherent in the structure and function of the multinational firm as a form of economic organization, or involving intergovernmental and intersocietal differences of perception and policy with respect to important domestic and international issues. As we proceed, we shall attempt to complete the matrix by identifying each of the major policy targets, assess its characteristics on the basis of available evidence, and match it to the form of multinational corporate behavior that seems most appropriate.

COMPLIANCE-ORIENTED BEHAVIOR

Strict adherence to legal and administrative constraints and to the rules of the marketplace, without substantial voluntarism, seems to make sense in a number of conflict situations. Allegations of social irresponsibility have been raised in each instance, but the solutions would appear to lie largely with the relevant national regulatory framework.

Financial Market Instability

One area of criticism strongly adverse to multinational firms, especially in the early 1970s, involves their operations in foreign exchange and short-term money markets. With substantial working capital balances, payables and receivables denominated in various currencies at any one time, multinational companies as a group are often considered to be a potentially destabilizing force in the international financial system.[21] By taking short positions in currencies they feel are weak and long positions in particularly strong currencies, they allegedly have the power to bring about the very exchange-rate shifts they expect. And, to the extent expectations are exaggerated or simply wrong, such behavior tends to accentuate fluctuations and uncertainty in foreign-exchange markets, increases the cost of hedging, and damages orderly flows of international trade investment. Prior to 1971 there was little to discourage such behavior, because under government-pegged exchange rates there was little chance of loss; since then, with exchange rates largely determined by the market, the chances of gain and loss are much more symmetrical.

There is little doubt that multinational firms build exchange-rate expectations into their international money management, moving funds around in accordance with these expectations. However, the reward structures of corporate financial officers seem to be rather "defense biased" (reducing the perceived likelihood of loss) instead of "offense biased" (actively seeking windfall gains), and if the multinationals have indeed been playing this game "offensively" they have been seriously suboptimizing.[22] Moreover, they are not alone; their short-term international funds movements have been paralleled by wealthy individuals, small-country governments and, more recently, by the oil exporting nations. Together, these forces have introduced unprecedented potential for short-term instability into international financial markets. Still, under the current system of floating exchange rates, this potential for instability and disruption has not been realized to the extent feared. With few exceptions, foreign-exchange risk has been kept within reasonable bounds, while international trade and finance have grown apace.

It is difficult to conclude that this aspect of multinational corporate behavior has very much to do with social responsibility. The firm plays according to the rules, as does everyone else, and disruptive behavior is largely a matter of shortcomings in the rules of the game. Alignment of foreign-exchange behavior to national and international economic requirements is a matter for intergovernmental agreement, and there seems little reason to suggest that firms should adopt policies other than those deriving from the dictates of optimum multinational cash management.

Tax Avoidance

A similar conclusion can be reached perhaps more arguably in the case of international taxation. Like an individual, a firm seeks to minimize the overall tax burden in order to maximize after-tax earnings that are available for reinvestment or distribution to share-holders. Unlike national enterprises—and ruling out the possibility of illegal action through tax evasion—the multinational firm's opportunities for tax avoidance are alleged to be substantial as a result of international differences in fiscal levies and inconsistencies in tax laws. Governments may levy taxes only on profits repatriated to the home country, not on global earnings. Retained earnings and dividends may be subject to different tax rates. Taxes paid to foreign governments may be taken as a credit against domestic tax liabilities or as a deduction. Various tax-credit and depreciation schemes may apply, as well as assorted tax holidays. Once the firm has figured out how to minimize its global tax liability within existing constraints, it may be possible to shift funds explicitly, or through transfer pricing, intrafirm royalty and fee payments, and other transactions to low-tax countries in order to substantially meet this objective.[23] Spokesmen for multinational companies often deny this, and tax avoidance undoubtedly varies widely between firms. But general denial seems futile in view of the widespread establishment of multinational corporate units in low-tax countries which are otherwise difficult to justify.

Social responsibility in the tax field surely involves adherence to all applicable laws and regulations and conformity with the "tax morality" prevailing in each country. But conflict is inherent in the field of taxation, and this is compounded at the international level. Home- and host-countries can be expected to close whatever loopholes existing regulatory capabilities permit. But many of the problems of tax avoidance cannot be resolved unilaterally, and will require inter-governmental agreement and mutual enforcement. Even then, conflict will arise between governments on the distribution of revenues. Nevertheless, taxation of multinational corporations is one of the few areas—perhaps the only one—where international uniformity in behavioral constraints makes sense. International agreements that may in the end raise the incidence of multinational corporate taxation seem both desirable and inevitable, and companies must plan for them and abide by them once they are instituted. However, they need not, as a matter of social responsibility, anticipate them.

Competitive Laxity

Because of their often extraordinary locational flexibility it is alleged that multinational companies are able to induce host governments to implement policies much more favorable to the firm than can reasonably be justified—and/or more favorable than apply to locally owned enterprises. At the entry level, this may consist of government grants and loans, concessionary credit terms, tax holidays of varying duration, zoning variances, duty-free imports, wage-rate ceilings, guarantees of labor tranquility, assured earnings remissions, or concessionary freight rates. Such factors appear to be less important when the investment is intended to serve the local market than when it is export oriented.

In extreme cases, the firm seeking a low labor cost "export platform" may shop around for a time among four or five countries having competitive labor-market conditions, transportation facilities, and the like, and enter into preliminary discussion with the respective governments. Depending on their need for the facility in question, the governments may "bid" for it using terms and conditions governing the investment as inducements. The firm may help matters along through selective communications with its negotiating partners, and the ultimate outcome may be far better for the firm (and worse for the country) than it had any right to expect.[24] The problem may be especially acute for some developing countries with inherently weak bargaining positions.

While this kind of exercise may be hard to resist, given the firm's bargaining position, at least in making the initial investment, moderation may well be the best counsel. Once the firm is committed, however, relative leverage usually shifts in favor of the host country. Extortionate or overly generous entry terms may later create an atmosphere of ill will that can backfire, particularly if they deprive government of policy tools that may be needed in the future to cope with changing economic or social conditions. Although hard bargaining does not imply social irresponsibility, bargaining outcomes may be viewed differently in retrospect and can fundamentally affect long-range assessments of the social value of the multinational firm.[25] The firm itself has to decide whether it is wise to press for maximum concessions in the short run if this runs the risk of a serious backlash later on.

Competition

Multinational firms often are accused of impairing competitive conditions in national markets to the detriment of productive efficiency and economic welfare in host countries. The argument runs as follows: By virtue of their superior management, marketing, product quality, and financial strength, they are able to gain in market share at the expense of local firms, reducing the number of surviving enterprises and lessening effective competition. They may also negotiate high rates of protection from competitive imports, thereby perhaps securing for themselves monopoly positions, and maintain arrangements not to compete with the parent or other affiliates in export markets.[26]

Increasing concentration in major industrial sectors and multinational corporate involvement today concerns governmental authorities in many countries, although conditions of competition are not the same as perhaps they once were. Beyond some minimum, the *number* of firms may not say very much about competitive behavior, particularly when there is vigorous import competition in addition to indigenous suppliers.[27] Indeed, some countries have actively promoted mergers and consolidations among locally owned enterprises where market definition extended well beyond national boundaries. A recent study shows that, on balance, subsidiaries of foreign firms in the Canadian and Australian markets tend to *increase* effective competition, allocative efficiency, and technical advancement.[28] There is also increasingly vigorous (if imperfect) antitrust enforcement and public regulation, as social controls partly take over the role of the classic competitive market.

Paradoxically, multinational firms have also been accused of creating "excessive" competition in national markets. Once a firm decides to enter a market or expand operations based on expectations of growth and profitability, multinational competitors may do likewise in an effort to maintain global market share. This "bandwagon effect" may make little economic sense, and indeed may lead to too many producers, each operating inefficiently, competing for a market of limited size. Resources are used inefficiently, and when the eventual shakeout comes the survivors may consist largely of multinational affiliates. Even then, the number of competitors may be excessive, but withdrawal remains difficult for managers looking at global market strategy.

Competitive relationships, although they play an important role in defining the net contribution of the multinational firm to national welfare, remain largely outside the scope of corporate voluntarism, and social control remains squarely in the realm of public policy.

Eroding the Labor Base

Arguments similar to the foregoing are frequently applied to principal factors of production as well. On the labor side, by paying highly competitive wages and fringe benefits, and providing superior working conditions, job security, and prospects for advancement, the multinationals are sometimes alleged to skim the cream off the local labor force, thereby weakening productivity in locally owned businesses and eroding their competitive position. Sometimes they also promote emigration of skilled people to new employment in the parent firm or third-country affiliates. The result may be increased foreign domination of industry and external dependence of the national economy and inhibited development of indigenous human resources and entrepreneurship.[29]

The argument seems plausible, but its validity depends on the circumstances involved. Multinational firms in some host countries absorb only a small fraction of the labor force and have considerable employment turnover, so that the quality and quantity of labor available to local firms may be affected only marginally, if at all. Labor quality may actually rise due to the training provided by foreign affiliates to workers who subsequently leave to start their own businesses or join local firms. In other cases the alternative to employment by multinationals may not be equivalent employment by local industry, but unemployment or underemployment. A decision then has to be made whether to play the multinationals' game or leave people unemployed or less productively employed while local industry develops. Most countries faced with this choice at the margin have understandably taken the first option. While the incremental demand for labor created by foreign affiliates in host countries may give rise to problems for locally owned firms, the issue cannot be considered a matter of social responsibility.

Eroding the Capital Base

A parallel argument can be made on the capital side, namely, that multinationals tend to minimize their local equity exposure by obtaining a significant part of their initial capital needs locally, from government loans and grants or from the local capital market, and subsequently satisfy much of their working capital requirements from local borrowings as well. The superior credit standing of the multinational firms, combined with the desire in some cases of government to accommodate them wherever possible, is alleged to divert investible funds away from the indigenous business sector.

To the extent that multinationals are a major source of incremental demand in local capital markets, such allegations may have some merit. Their presence may drive up capital costs in general. At the same time, multinational affiliates may benefit from lower interest rates and more available credit than locally owned firms. Government capital disbursements to acquire land or construct facilities for multinationals may come at the expense of public investment in infrastructure or other alternatives. On the other hand, multinationals do provide an outlet for local capital that would otherwise be less efficiently put to use. In point of fact, it is exceedingly difficult to assess the capital-diverting impact of multinational firms in host countries. Recent studies have been contradictory and seem to indicate that foreign-owned enterprises in some host countries may be at least as important as *suppliers* of funds to local capital markets as they are on the demand side.[30] Again, the issue seems to call for minimal voluntary action on the part of the multinational enterprise. Company policy should be geared to normal competitive relationships in the financial sector within existing institutional constraints.

SELECTIVE VOLUNTARISM

Compliance-oriented behavior may be appropriate in a number of areas that are either relatively nonsensitive or where responsibility for setting behavioral constraints clearly appears to rest at the governmental level. There are, on the other hand, a number of sources of conflict that do demand voluntary action on the part of the enterprise. There is little evidence, however, to suggest that attempts to go beyond what is required—toward what is thought to be socially beneficial in the local environment—will in the end protect a firm from nationalization or expropriation. Such steps usually involve overriding ideological and national policy issues, balanced however imperfectly against a political and economic assessment of the costs associated with removal of foreign ownership. The political indictment of the firm will be tailored to achieve the desired end, rational or not. For the individual firm, at the margin, social responsibility does not appear to pay off in terms of longevity.[31] We should also note that socially irresponsible action by a single firm may trigger adverse reaction, not only upon the offending firm itself, but also upon other multinational firms which have consistently pursued a socially responsible course.

Exploitation of Labor

A common allegation against multinational companies is that they take advantage of local labor-market conditions and employ workers, particularly for export production, at wage rates far lower than could be obtained in the firm's home country or elsewhere. And affiliates of foreign-owned firms are sometimes accused of using their importance as employers to pay substandard wages and provide inadequate working conditions.

The first point cannot be challenged in cases where multinationals do take advantage of intercountry differences in the cost of labor in order to reduce overall production costs. The classic case is the for-eign-owned electronics plant in Taiwan or Malaysia employing local women in assembly of components, made of imported parts, for export and further processing or final assembly abroad—with the labor input comprising essentially all of the local value-added. Yet this is what international specialization and trade is all about, and the presence of multinationals in local labor markets usually drives up employment and wages far faster than otherwise would be the case. Everybody benefits—the local workers, the host country, the firm and its cus-tomers, with the possible exception of workers displaced in the firm's home country or elsewhere by offshore labor-intensive production. And even in the latter case the evidence, while contradictory, suggests that the transitional effect on wages and jobs may be less than is often assumed—especially when white-collar jobs are also taken into account.[32]

The second allegation, concerning exploitive wages and working conditions, is seldom even raised in the affected countries. The fact is that multinationals today usually pay higher wages, provide better fringe benefits, and maintain higher standards of plant safety and

worker health and nutrition than comparable locally owned enterprises.[33] They do this for competitive reasons, to attract the best people,
and because they are well aware of their vulnerability to charges of
labor exploitation. Socially responsible employment practices represent sound policy for the multinational firm in host countries, although
there seems to be a very thin line between adequacy and paternalism,
which in turn can eventually lead to conflict. Sensitivity to local
practices regarding layoffs, promotion, seniority, female employment,
labor negotiations, and the like is a problem for firms operating in
many national settings. Multinationals make mistakes, but they generally learn quickly and with relatively little friction. Labor relations is
an area that is both sensitive to charges of social irresponsibility and
often ill-defined in terms of external constraints, and hence multinational corporate voluntarism is a significant issue—particularly where
relatively new departures such as codetermination are involved.[34]

Expatriate Management

It is sometimes argued that managerial ranks in affiliates of multinational firms are the preserve of foreigners. This limits opportunities
for the advancement of local employees to more responsible positions
and stunts the development of an indigenous managerial and entre-
preneurial class. It also concentrates operating decisions that have an
important bearing on the host economy in the hands of expatriate
foreigners who may be unaware of, or insensitive to, local needs.

Such arguments are, as a rule, vacuous. Although there appear to be
differences among firms and between host countries, multinational
corporations today generally try to keep expatriate managerial involvement to the bare minimum needed for efficient operations.
Sometimes the expatriate contingent disappears altogether, but more
normally the extent of foreign involvement is reduced to a core group
consisting of the chief operating officer and one or two top associates,
with remainder of top and middle management staffed locally.[35] This
simply makes good business sense, at once reducing personnel costs,
providing incentives to local staff, and lessening the possibility of local

tension—especially with regard to salary differentials. Still, minimum expatriate involvement is a comparatively recent phenomenon, and the legacy of the past remains. And, with relatively few exceptions, the chances of locally recruited managers eventually finding themselves in the top ranks of the parent firm seem to be rather slight. Notwithstanding their strong record in this sensitive area, it is certainly advisable for multinationals to promote management opportunities for nationals of host countries to the fullest extent possible.

Environmental Safeguards

Another dimension of social responsibility concerns the natural environment. Pollution control policies differ widely among countries, ranging from strict regulation of environmental characteristics of production processes to no regulation at all—and even positive encouragement of new, pollutive industrial development. There are tradeoffs between environment and development that are determined politically by each country and may swing rather abruptly.[36] Because of this, multinational firms at a minimum adhere strictly to local regulations. Indeed, they often exceed them by wide margins, applying pollution standards that they have already had to meet elsewhere, and ultimately may develop an advantage over local firms in a period of tightening environmental controls. There have even been cases, as in the Malaysian timber industry, where multinationals may actually be favored over local firms because of their greater experience with environmental protection and their greater financial ability to pursue environmentally sound operations.

Environmental errors are made, of course—many of them difficult to reverse—and multinational corporations often are involved. There is generally plenty of blame to go around, and the multinational firm can expect to share disproportionately in that blame. Managers know this, and not infrequently seem to be more environmentally scrupulous abroad than at home. At the same time, there is little evidence that they tend to seek out "pollution havens," partly for the reason just cited and partly because environmental factors simply are not important enough, relative to other considerations, to determine plant-siting decisions even in the most pollutive industries.[37]

Consumer Protection

Closely related is the question of socially responsible behavior in the marketplace. There are wide variations between countries in laws and regulations governing advertising, packaging and labeling, product quality, credit terms, after-sales service, and other aspects of marketing—and often they are absent entirely. Alleged excesses, such as failure to inform users of possibly harmful side effects of certain drugs, or marketing shoddy merchandise in developing countries, are vehemently denied by industry. The problem is serious because coherent guidelines for socially responsible action in this field are often vague or nonexistent and because responsible marketing may involve substantial cost penalties.

There is very little evidence so far on this aspect of multinational corporate operations, although criticism abounds.[38] Unlike other dimensions of social responsibility, marketing practices frequently are not associated with a major "stake" by the firm in the local economy, such as a large fixed investment, and this may limit the possibility of effective sanctions by local authorities as well as the incentive for self-discipline. Moreover, there is room for argument on what should be marketed where and how; what people think they want is often at variance with what corporate executives or social critics think they ought to want. Certainly, compliant corporate behavior to conform strictly with local requirements is no guarantee against charges of social irresponsibility in the marketing area, and even uniform adherence to the strictest requirements encountered anywhere in a firm's multinational experience cannot prevent conflict when views differ radically between countries and over time.

Operational Instability and Speed of Adjustment

A comparatively recent view is that the range of locational options available to multinational companies makes them inherently less stable than comparable national firms. When political instability develops, or unit labor costs rise locally (or decline elsewhere), or a government adopts policies unfavorable to the multinational firm, it may simply pull out and seek greener pastures elsewhere. The country, meanwhile, may have shifted resources into this sector—often at great cost—only to see them expelled again at further cost to society and considerable trauma for those most directly affected. Such instability clearly diminishes the value of a particular foreign-investment project to the host country and, if confirmed, should be taken into account in formulating national policies toward multinational enterprises.

Available evidence, while tentative, seems to suggest that multinational corporate operations in some instances do indeed evidence instability, particularly in highly labor-intensive production. The "threshold" beyond which taxation or other cost-increasing policy measures may drive out foreign affiliates manufacturing garments, toys, or electronic components can be very low, and the rapidity with which the firm is able to disengage—particularly given modest fixed capital investment—can be astonishing.[39] Even with large fixed investment, as in the automotive industry, a firm with multiple plants in a given region can shift production if adverse conditions develop.

The multinational enterprise, as noted earlier, adapts quickly and efficiently to take advantage of changing production conditions, while the host countries and displaced productive factors must bear the principal adjustment burden. Multinational corporate involvement ties a country more closely to foreign swings in business conditions. Falling demand in major markets may prompt a firm to abandon manufacturing facilities in host countries while maintaining production in home and third-country plants. Such considerations have made it increasingly necessary for host countries to be circumspect about the "portfolio" of direct foreign investment by multinationals they seek to attract, considering the *instability risks* as well as the net *developmental benefits* that are likely to result.

More generally, we have identified as one of the multinational's chief contributions the general shortening of the adjustment period in the international economy, and a commensurate reduction in the gains from trade and specialization foregone during lengthy periods of economic adaptation. It has also increased the *cost* of adjustment to economic change at the national level, because the cost of adjustment tends to be inversely related to the time available for adaptation. An electronics plant in Singapore that ceases production and moves the short distance to Penang, Malaysia, where wage rates are lower can cause severe trauma on both ends—in Singapore by suddenly releasing thousands of specialized, semiskilled, mostly female workers, and in Penang by entering as a major new force in a sensitive labor market, with a large part of the immediate manpower needs met at the expense of existing firms. The multinational firm, its shareholders, its customers, suppliers and ultimately the consumers, as well as the new host economy, are the beneficiaries of such a shift, while the displaced workers and the impacted local economies bear most of the cost.

To limit the multinational's flexibility would be to limit its contribution to the international economy. But a strong case can be made for a more equitable sharing of the adjustment costs. The host government could dictate terms, including contract guarantees and escrow accounts for adjustment assistance. At the limit, precipitous behavior could lead to outright nationalization or expropriation. Moreover, multinational companies can enhance their value to host countries, and in addition reduce the potential for friction, by making a clear commitment to locational and operational stability from the outset.

Technological Adaptation

Multinational enterprise is frequently accused of failing to adapt technology to conditions (especially labor conditions) in countries in which it operates.[40] Not only does the technology used by many multinationals in manufacturing operations tend to be capital intensive in nature, providing only nominal incremental employment, but by driving out less technically advanced competitors the net impact may actually be to displace jobs. Especially in developing countries plagued by high unemployment and underemployment, some observers contend, not enough is done to adapt technology to local conditions in order to increase the labor content of production. They also maintain that this can be done without significant efficiency losses.[41]

The issue is debatable. On the one hand, much export-oriented foreign direct investment especially in developing countries is in fact highly labor intensive, and there is some question whether the labor-displacement hypothesis is indeed valid in the aggregate when all such operations are taken into account. It is certainly true that more labor-intensive technology could in some cases be used, but often this is contrained by the engineering characteristics of the production process (e.g., synthetic fibers or petrochemicals), and limited primarily to materials-handling operations.[42] Process adaptation could also raise unit costs or reduce product quality levels. Not least important, the use of less capital-intensive technology may imply built-in obsolescence and lower productivity, which could generate a different kind of conflict between the firm and host-country government. Indeed, proposals to meet the problem by applying technology that is obsolete (but more labor intensive) have often met with fierce resistance on the part of host countries—if only for reasons of national prestige.

While adaptation of production technology is an important social issue, no similar debate focuses on technology embodied in products sold in national markets. Here most countries want the latest and the best, and the ability to provide this on a continuing basis is considered an important contribution of multinational enterprise. In many cases, product adaptation to local conditions is both feasible and profitable, and a misreading of the market becomes evident very quickly. But there is ample potential for conflict, for instance, concerning the nature of products sold, pricing policy, and the amortization of research and development costs. Often the incremental manufacturing cost of products, as in the pharmaceuticals industry, is far below its full cost and governments, especially in poor countries, maintain that full-cost pricing is inequitable based on ability to pay. Price ceilings frequently have been introduced, for example, and it is difficult for the multinational firm in a competitive environment to abstain from marginal sales under such conditions.

Foreign Ownership

Much of the debate on multinational enterprise focuses on ownership of the means of production. Strong socialist factions in many countries are hostile to private enterprise on ideological grounds, and nationalist sentiment equating ownership with control, control with dependence, and dependence with loss of sovereignty may be equally hostile. For whatever reason, foreign ownership by itself, regardless of the net costs and benefits associated with it, has become a matter of contention that can seriously escalate conflicts between nation and firm that arise for substantive reasons.[43] It is highly volatile and is influenced by the vagaries of international politics. And it differs considerably between types of industries, with national defense, public utilities, banking, transport, and extractive sectors usually considered "sensitive," together with high-prestige domestic firms. Lastly, it is often complicated by national policy concerning participative management and industrial democracy, income and wealth redistribution, and other basic social trends that have little to do with multinational corporate behavior.

In many cases, aversion on the part of national authorities to foreign ownership seems irrational when the relevant costs and benefits are objectively weighed. Other priorities such as reducing unemployment and elevating living standards should logically come first, leaving the ownership question to perhaps be settled later through negotiated divestiture or nationalization. Too often the pressures build to the point where nationalization or expropriation occurs as an exercise in irrationality, with both firm and nation losing out, and the ownership change by itself contributing little or nothing. Timely accommodation by both sides may lead to superior outcomes, but requires a flexible management attitude on such issues as joint ventures, government participation, management contracts, licensing, and technical assistance. Managerial style and corporate image also may play an important role. As they have shown in Eastern Europe, multinational firms are not reluctant to explore a wide range of options, some of them unprecedented, when they have no choice. Increased flexibility on the part of firms in this respect may have positive value—multinational business can take many forms, and controlling equity participation is only one alternative.[44]

AVOIDANCE-ORIENTED BEHAVIOR

There are, finally, some important sources of conflict between the multinational firm and the national state that cannot be alleviated either by strict compliance with externally imposed constraints or through voluntary alignment of corporate policies with prevailing social objectives. These arise in part from the fundamental characteristics of multinationalism, and there is usually very little the firm can do but try to avoid the source of the problem, maintain a low profile, or engage in open and honest debate on the merits of the issue at hand.

Cultural Erosion

One of the less tangible sources of conflict surrounding the multinational enterprise is its impact on patterns of living. By introducing from abroad new products and new ways of doing things, it is alleged that the firm undermines local culture and promotes an international sameness that eventually swamps cultural diversity. Modern industrial societies generally end up adopting similar basic patterns of work—including regular hours, hierarchical organizations, repetitive tasks, and achievement orientation—as well as common consumption patterns, leisure, dress, even language. Although the basic cultural identity may remain partially intact, many of the less desirable aspects of industrial development seem inevitable—urban sprawl, traffic congestion, and increased tension are often mentioned.

The role of the multinational enterprise in cultural erosion is that of accelerator. Other transmission mechanisms, such as trade, tourism, and the media work as effectively, if more gradually. This shows up quite clearly in comparisons of changes in life styles between the countries of Eastern Europe (with little multinational corporate involvement) and Western Europe. Frequently, too, the firm will try to adapt products and processes to local conditions in ways that minimize cultural disruption, simply because it makes good business sense. However unfortunate, cultural change accompanies economic growth, and such tradeoffs must be taken into consideration in national development planning, whether or not this involves multinational enterprise. The latter is fundamentally identified with economic and social dynamism and cannot escape being associated with cultural change.

Erosion of Economic Policy

The nature of multinational corporate operations and their flexibility are viewed as potential underminers of effective national economic policy. Underinvoicing of exports of goods and services and overinvoicing of imports, within and between firms, can be used to erode exchange control and liquidate blocked financial balances. Microeconomic controls over prices, production, stockpiling, raw materials, credit, transport, and the like can be evaded through bribery and other illicit transactions. Wherever command-type economic controls exist, for whatever reason, the incentive to evade exists as well.[45] There is no available evidence that multinational firms behave more or less responsibly under such circumstances than indigenous firms. At the margin one might suspect that they behave with more restraint in the face of domestic controls (in spite of their greater evasive potential) because of a more exposed position, and less responsibly on exchange controls because the incentive to export funds—and the opportunity to do so—may be greater for the typical multinational firm than for comparable locally owned firms.

Perhaps less immediately confrontive is the view that multinationals are also able to avoid the effects of macroeconomic policy, thereby undermining governments' control over the general price level, unemployment, and other macro-variables. The so-called escape hypothesis says that affiliates of multinational firms can avoid domestic credit restraint by obtaining external finance, either from the parent or from the international capital market, sources normally closed to local firms. Restrictive fiscal policy can be similarly avoided, for example, by simply shifting output to export markets. At the extreme, this view holds that the expanding role of multinational firms has cost nation-states control of their own economic destinies and has paralyzed governments in coming to grips with inflation and recession in the mid-1970s.[46]

The escape hypothesis is intuitively appealing, but exceedingly difficult to substantiate. The only systematic studies to date that compare the reactions of multinational affiliates with local firms to credit restraint present a very mixed picture that is not at all convincing one way or the other.[47] Except where "moral suasion" and similar techniques are part of accepted macroeconomic polity, however, it is difficult to ascribe the escape phenomenon—if it exists—to social irresponsibility of the multinational firm.

Research and Development

Another allegation is that multinational enterprise concentrates its research and development activities at corporate headquarters, or in a few major research centers, but rarely does significant research in host countries. This limits the benefits to the host country by "stunting" its technological development, limiting job opportunities for research-oriented graduates of educational institutions, forcing its best researchers to emigrate, building in a balance-of-payments burden by requiring substantial monetary disbursements for foreign technology—while receiving little if anything for domestically developed technology used abroad—and institutionalizing technological dependence.

Multinational firms do not, in fact, do significant amounts of *basic* research in all of their foreign affiliates. This is less true in advanced nations (especially in the United States and Western Europe) than in developing host countries.[48] Basic R & D usually requires an advanced technological environment with substantial exchanges of ideas between universities, research institutes, government agencies, professional associations, and other firms. There may also be significant scale economies in R & D activities, which would necessitate concentration of this function within the firm. Such factors preclude decentralization or dispersion of large-scale research, except perhaps where major free-standing divisions of a multinational company are headquartered abroad. Firms seek to concentrate research where this can be accomplished most effectively and efficiently, and this coincides with their general contribution to international specialization and division of labor. Even with the rapid intrafirm dissemination of technical advances, however, they will not escape criticism on this account. On the other hand, they may be able to point to significant ongoing *applied* research aimed at adapting products and processes to local conditions, which is often carried out on site.

Managerial Extraterritoriality

One major source of conflict endemic to multinational corporate operations is the fact that basic decisions are taken abroad. Such decisions may dictate, for example, closure of a plant or expansion or contraction of output at a particular production site. They may concern shifts in plant location; production for export; or imports of finished goods, raw materials, and components—all of which tend to be of particular interest to host-country governments. Or they may involve alteration of pricing or advertising policy, or of the product mix.

It is clear that managerial objectives and priorities do not necessarily coincide with those of host countries and that there may be some slippage of sensitivity to local needs in headquarters-level decisions. Foreign ownership or control of the means of production thus tends to be associated with a loss of national sovereignty, as we have already noted. The real question is how different such decisions would be if local ownership or control prevailed—whether management under such circumstances would respond differently to local needs and preferences. Often the outcome undoubtedly would differ, but at a cost. If a strong nationalist sentiment is prevalent, particularly among the elites, pressure may develop for reassertion of national prerogatives regardless of any other elements in the case.

Some multinational firms appear to be working to advance management sensitivity to local conditions by improving communications between parent and affiliate, reducing reaction times, and increasing the degree of local autonomy in critical areas.[49] But the underlying possibility of conflict between corporate and national objectives remains and will invariably result from time to time in an atmosphere of confrontation.

Political Extraterritoriality and Involvement

A related area of potential conflict involves both encroachment on the political sovereignty of one nation by another through the multinational enterprise and enhanced corporate economic leverage through home-country political backing.

Company affiliates in various countries do business under local laws and regulations, and almost always are considered legal persons through incorporation with limited liability. The host country expects conformity with prevailing domestic and foreign policies both of locally owned firms and foreign affiliates. The multinational firm, on the other hand, may be under pressure from its home government, the media, or special-interest groups to force its affiliates to behave according to standards prevailing at home or some "higher" moral or ethical values.

Policies of the host country may be considered harmful to the home nation's military or political interests—an example often cited is the U.S. Transaction Control Regulations of 1953, which prohibits American firms *and their foreign affiliates* from engaging in trade with socialist countries in a range of sensitive products.[50] An American-owned firm in England or Canada could thus be prevented from exporting to Cuba or the Soviet Union, even though such action might be perfectly legal and indeed desirable in the United Kingdom. Another popular example involves American firms in South Africa, which encounter conflicting pressures ranging from total withdrawal to upgrading working conditions of nonwhites beyond those prevailing in locally owned firms.[51] The oil crisis of 1973–74 provides another example, with the multinational oil companies redirecting crude and product shipments among embargoed and nonembargoed countries to minimize disruptions while simultaneously seeking not to cross the political objectives of Arab oil exporters. And there is the Arab "blacklist" of firms doing business with Israel which, as expected, contains a large number of multinationals.

International conflicts in public policy present an insoluble problem for the multinational firm, since adaptive behavior, which we have tried to argue normally minimizes the risk of social irresponsibility, is in fact the *source* of conflict. The dimensions of the problem grow even more serious in a dynamic context, when past firm behavior is viewed in retrospect as intercountry conflicts change through time. In the extreme case, the firm may be considered an "agent" of its home government and may be subject to adverse reactions quite unjustified by its overall performance in the host country. Conversely, it may be viewed as receiving implicit or explicit support from its home government when conflicts develop. Using their political leverage, the home governments may bring to bear pressure on behalf of "their" multinationals in the hope of achieving bargaining outcomes superior to what the firms could achieve on their own—and superior to what indigenous firms can attain—and possibly adverse to the interests of the host country itself.

Multinationals may use all of the instruments at their disposal in their dealings with host governments. This sometimes includes the good offices of the home government's local diplomatic presence. There is nothing wrong with this so long as it does not involve interference by a foreign government in the internal affairs of a sovereign state. No country can or should tolerate such behavior, and it will almost certainly harm the basic interests of the initiating firm and other multinationals in the end. Isolated transgressions in this area in the past have done greater and more lasting damage to the interests of multinational firms than any other issue discussed here. The failure of other multinationals to unite in castigating and disassociating themselves publicly from these transgressions has created an atmosphere of sinister brotherhood and conspiracy that, although it may be false, is likely to take generations to overcome—indeed, for practical purposes, may be irreparable. Fortunately, restraint is now the watchword of home governments, and there remains little political support for interventionist action except in the case of expropriations and nationalization with patently inadequate compensation.[52] The firm is having to fight its own battles and argue the issues on their merits.

CONCLUSIONS

In one sense, our discussion has been addressed to managers of multinational firms at all levels—managers who have to make the day-to-day decisions that commit the enterprise to courses of action which may or may not be considered socially responsible by the outside world. Management has ways of avoiding conflict, but there is no way of avoiding decisions. We have accepted the view that social responsibility extends *beyond* classic profit-maximizing behavior within externally imposed constraints, to encompass long-term corporate viability in a transnational economic environment as an integral component of business planning. Reconciliation of societal and corporate goals and objectives at minimum cost requires formulation of usable corporate decision rules. We have proposed a framework for doing that, based on a taxonomy of conflict sources grouped according to the apparent efficacy of compliant, voluntary, or avoidance-oriented behavior. One can perhaps argue with the results, and with the evidence presented on the issues. But one cannot argue with the ultimate need to *share* responsibility for social improvement between firms that are basically economic entities and the political decision process. For management, this means sensitivity in the assignment of instruments of corporate policy to those targets that are most responsive to them, and careful avoidance of conflict situations that cannot be resolved by its own actions. The lessons are important, and there is growing evidence suggesting that many of today's attitudes on the part of management toward social responsibility were nurtured among affiliates abroad and fed back into headquarters thinking under pressure from international executives on the line.

In a quite different sense, the discussion is also addressed to external observers of the multinational firm, in an attempt to present a balanced view of the scope and limits of corporate social responsibility. The discussion has purposely focused on fundamental aspects of multinational business and their relationships to major social objectives because this is where the control conflict lies. Good "corporate citizenship" defined at the community level is also important; but it is not decisive. Very basic issues concerning jobs, income, technology, management, taxes, and political sovereignty define the value of the international firm to the national state and will, in the end, decide its fate. People need to know what these issues are, how multinational firms affect them, and what options appear to be available for conflict resolution.

A critical need is much more extensive and candid disclosure of corporate operations and policies. Inadequacy of hard evidence is perhaps the principal (and largely unnecessary) source of confusion and misunderstanding surrounding the multinational enterprise. It is difficult to argue "efficiency" in the collection, organization, and use of information as one of the principal social benefits associated with multinational firms, when there is clearly inadequate *reverse flow* of information to the external environment for the sake of maintaining competitive advantages. Firms have for too long been allowed to hide behind the "proprietory" nature of information on prices, finance, production, taxes, staffing, and the like.[53] If they fail to move ahead meaningfully on their own, disclosure requirements imposed from without—which will surely involve substantial disruptions and compliance costs—are a virtual certainty. It is only a matter of time before effective "transparency" of the multinational firm is a fact of life.

It is also important for multinationals to rise more effectively and objectively to their own defense. They must cease simply reacting to outside pressures and begin to take the initiative in explaining themselves in terms of social benefits and costs to those holding a public mandate to safeguard the national interest. Far too much reliance is placed on often nefarious political lobbying activities, and on discussion within traditional business forums, where the multinationals always succeed in reinforcing their own views and sometimes succeed in influencing contemporary political decision makers, but rarely develop needed broad-based political support. Much of this activity has long since lost credibility and is often positively counterproductive. And when it oversteps increasingly apparent limits to acceptable conduct (even on the part of a single firm), the political reaction can be both severe and lasting. Especially in host countries, multinational managers have been surprisingly reluctant to speak out in public debate—even when their positions are eminently defensible.

People are skeptical. They worry about the multinationals' power and impact on their daily lives. They identify the multinational firm with maintenance of the status quo, working against what is viewed as beneficial economic and social change in the public sector even as it creates dramatic change in the private sector. What is needed is a forthright and continuing dialogue on the issues, based on adequate information, in order to generate a composite image of the multinational enterprise that adequately and credibly reflects the reality.[54]

Can multinational business be relied upon systematically to pursue socially responsible courses of actions, or must we turn to increasingly powerful external control by governments that channel the creative drive of the firm in predetermined directions and simultaneously close off some of its options? Which is more efficient? Which will address more effectively the growing interdependence of economics and politics and deal more humanely with the changing needs of the evolving international economic order?

Multinational enterprise as a form of economic organization is hardly sacrosanct. It is a *tool,* nothing more, to be used by society in the achievement of whatever objectives it sets for itself. It will be retained only as long as the perceived social benefits it throws off exceed the perceived social costs associated with its existence. Otherwise, one way or another, it will be discarded. Sensitive and adaptive corporate social responsibility, put into practice with careful attention to the policy-assignment dimension emphasized here, can help assure its survival.

NOTES

Acknowledgments: An earlier version of this essay was widely circulated. Although they bear no responsibility for the final product, helpful comments and criticisms by Douglas Adkins, Edward Altman, William Baumol, Ronald Danielian, William Dill, John Dutton, Donald Guertin, Robert Hawkins, Ashok Kapoor, Robert Kavesh, Richard Levich, Tracy Murray, Walter Ness, Alex Rathe, Larry Ritter, Arnold Sametz, and Terry Sanders are gratefully acknowledged.

1. For a first-rate survey, see C. Fred Bergsten, ed., *The Future of the International Economic Order: An Agenda for Research* (Lexington, Mass.: D.C. Heath, 1973).
2. A recent, heavily promoted example is Richard J. Barnet and Ronald E. Müller, *Global Reach* (New York: Simon and Schuster, 1975). This volume is poorly researched, often sloppy and sometimes intellectually dishonest in a passionate search for a telling indictment of the multinational firm as a form of economic organization and its managers as human beings. It nevertheless contains occasional flashes of insight and raises once again a number of questions, all of them raised before, that will have to be answered through balanced and careful scholarship, together with economic and political statesmanship.
3. Cf. the papers contained in Charles P. Kindleberger, ed., *The International Corporation* (Cambridge, Mass.: MIT Press, 1970).
4. For an elaboration, see John H. Dunning, "Determinants of International Production," *Oxford Economic Papers* (November 1973).
5. This point is discussed in Robert G. Hawkins, "International Firms and the Economic Development of Developing Countries," in S. Chee and K. S. Mun, eds., *Malaysia and the Multinational Corporations* (Kuala Lumpur: Malaysian Economic Association, 1974).
6. See John Stopford and Louis T. Wells, *Managing the Multinational Corporation* (New York: Basic Books, 1973).
7. Much the same problem exists in the general theory of the firm and the use of standard microeconomic analysis to predict economic behavior.

But perhaps the issue is somewhat more serious when the firm is operating in a discontinuous international environment.

8. For an excellent discussion, see Raymond Vernon, *Sovereignty at Bay* (New York: Basic Books, 1972).

9. See, for example, Howard R. Bowen, *Social Responsibilities of the Businessman* (New York: Harper & Brothers, 1953); and, more recently, Peter F. Drucker, *Management: Tasks, Responsibilities, Practices* (New York: Harper & Row, 1974). See also Earl F. Cheit, ed., *The Business Establishment* (New York: Wiley, 1964); and Richard Eells and Clarence Walton, *Conceptual Foundations of Business* (Homewood, Ill.: Richard D. Irwin, 1969).

10. Some observers support this view for the opposite reason. They profess absolutely no confidence in business voluntarism and prefer government policies that *force* profit-maximizing firms to assume social responsibility. See William J. Baumol, "Business Morality and the Social Interest: Smith vs. Marx," New York University Center for Applied Economics, Discussion Paper No. 74-07 (mimeograph), April 1974. For the other view, see especially Milton Friedman, *Capitalism and Freedom* (Chicago: University of Chicago Press, 1962); Friedrich A. Hayek, *The Road to Serfdom* (Chicago: University of Chicago Press, 1944); and Theodore Levitt, "The Dangers of Social Responsibility," *Harvard Business Review* (September–October 1958).

11. See Joseph W. McGuire, *Business and Society* (New York: McGraw-Hill, 1963) for an excellent survey of the issues involved. Also Neil W. Chamberlain, *The Limits of Corporate Responsibility* (New York: Basic Books, 1973); George A. Smith, Jr., and John B. Mathews, *Business, Society, and the Individual* (Homewood, Ill.: Richard D. Irwin, 1967); and Edward S. Mason, ed., *The Corporation in Modern Society* (Cambridge, Mass.: Harvard University Press, 1960).

12. Cf. David A. Aaker and George S. Day, "Corporate Responses to Consumerism Pressures," *Harvard Business Review* (November–December 1972); Council on Environmental Quality, *Environmental Quality* (Washington, D.C.: U.S. Government Printing Office, 1975); and Committee for Economic Development, *Social Responsibility of Business Corporations* (New York: CED, 1971).

13. On the other hand, the same thing can be said of democracy vis-à-vis totalitarianism.

14. R. Coppock *et al.,* "Social Pressures and Business Actions," Battelle Seattle Research Center (mimeograph), November 1972.

15. Arthus M. Louis, "The View from the Pinnacle: What Business Thinks,"

Fortune (September 1969); and David Ewing, "Who Wants Corporate Democracy?" *Harvard Business Review* (September–October 1971). S. Prakash Sethi, ed., *Up Against the Corporate Wall: Modern Corporations and Social Issues* (Englewood Cliffs N.J.: Prentice-Hall, 1971).

16. Quoted in Leonard Silk, "Multinational Morals," *New York Times,* March 5, 1974, p. 33.

17. See ORC Public Opinion Index, "Social Activists' Views on Business and the Role of Corporate Boards of Directors," Opinion Research Corporation, April 1974.

18. An even finer breakdown has been suggested in correspondence by W. R. Dill: (a) Adaptive/passive: sensitivity to social issues and avoidance of friction while watching out for corporate interests. (b) Passive-/avoidance: adapt when forced to do so but otherwise maintain a low profile. (c) Adaptive/assertive: sensitivity to social issues coupled to a willingness to join the debate on the character of the firm's regulatory environment. (d) Assertive/missionary: sensitivity to social issues combined with an honest and actively expressed belief that social welfare is best served through multinational corporate influence on world governmental structures. (e) Assertive/acquisitive: minimal sensitivity—the name of the game is free enterprise in an environment where outcomes are determined by the exercise of raw economic and political power.

19. For an earlier version of this thesis applied to a specific case, see my "Foreign Subsidiary Operations: Adverse Reaction and MNC Response," in S. Chee and K.S. Mun, eds., *op. cit.*

20. For an interesting discussion, see John Kenneth Galbraith, "Power and the Useful Economist," *American Economic Review* (March 1973); and of course his *The New Industrial State,* rev. ed. (Boston: Houghton Mifflin, 1972).

21. For a shrill indictment, see Richard Barnet and Ronald Müller, *op. cit.;* a more reasoned assessment, with a good deal of evidence, is contained in Sidney M. Robbins and Robert B. Stobaugh, *Money in Multinational Enterprise* (New York: Basic Books, 1972). Another recent study is Benjamin Klein, *The Role of U.S. Multinational Corporations in Recent Exchange Crises* (Washington, D.C.: Center for Multinational Studies Occasional Paper No. 6, December 1974).

22. See M. Z. Brooke and H. L. Remmers, *The Strategy of Multinational Enterprise* (London: Longmans, 1970); and E. M. Bernstein, "Multinational Corporation and the Exchange Crises," testimony before the U.N. Commission on Multinational Enterprise, September 1973 (mimeograph).

23. See S. Lall, "Transfer Pricing by Multinational Manufacturing Firms," *Oxford Bulletin of Economics and Statistics* (August 1973); Thomas Horst, "The Theory of the Multinational Firm: Optimal Behavior Under Different Tariff and Tax Rates," *Journal of Political Economy* (September 1971); and J. Schulman, "When Price Is Wrong by Design," *Columbia Journal of World Business* (May–June 1967). An excellent recent work is Constantine V. Vaitsos, *Intercountry Income Distribution and Transnational Enterprise* (London: Oxford University Press, 1974).

24. Cf. Edith Penrose, *The Large International Firm in Developing Countries* (London: Allen & Unwin, 1967). Also G. L. Reuber *et al.*, *Private Foreign Investment in Development* (New York: Oxford University Press, 1973).

25. For some case studies see Ashok Kapoor, *International Business Negotiations* (New York: New York University Press, 1970); and his *The Negotiation Era and the Multinational Enterprise* (New York: Ballinger, 1974).

26. See United Nations Conference on Trade and Development, *Restrictive Business Practices* (Geneva: UNCTAD document TD/122/Supp. 1, 1972).

27. A clear discussion is contained in F. M. Scherer, *Industrial Pricing: Theory and Evidence* (Chicago: Rand McNally, 1974).

28. Richard E. Caves, "Multinational Firms, Competition, and Productivity in Host-Country Markets," *Economica* (May 1974); and his "International Corporations: The Industrial Economics of Foreign Investment," *Economica* (March 1971).

29. Cf. G. L. Reuber *et al.*, *op. cit.* The counterpart argument of multinational corporate "exploitation" of labor in host countries is discussed below.

30. See, for example, Falih Alsaaty, "Foreign Investment and Economic Development in the Philippines," unpublished Ph.D. dissertation, New York University, 1972.

31. See Raymond Vernon, "Foreign Operations," in James W. McKie, ed., *Social Responsibility and the Business Predicament* (Washington, D.C.: The Brookings Institution, 1975). Also see Robert G. Hawkins, Norman Mintz, and Michael Provissiero, *Governmental Takeovers of U.S. Foreign Affiliates: A Postwar Profile* (Washington, D.C.: Center for Multinational Studies, Occasional Paper No. 7, 1975).

32. For a balanced account, see Robert G. Hawkins, "The Multinational Corporation: A New Trade Policy Issue in the United States," in R. G. Hawkins and I. Walter, eds., *The United States in International Markets* (Lexington, Mass.: D.C. Heath, 1972). See also R. B. Stobaugh *et al.*, "U.S. Multinational Enterprise and the U.S. Economy," in *The Multinational Corporation: Studies on U.S. Foreign Investment* (Washington, D.C.: Department of Commerce, 1972); and Duane Kujawa, ed., *Ameri-*

can Labor and the Multinational Corporation (New York: Praeger, 1973).

33. Cf. Duane Kujawa, *International Labor Relations Management in the Automotive Industry* (New York: Praeger, 1971).

34. See especially International Labor Office, *Multinational Enterprises and Social Policy* (Geneva: ILO, 1973).

35. See *ibid.* Also see Falih Alsaaty, *op. cit.,* and Okunle Iyanda, "A Socio-Economic Cost-Benefit Analysis of Foreign Direct Investment in Nigeria," unpublished Ph.D. dissertation, New York University, 1975. For an earlier discussion, see John Fayerweather, *Management of International Operations* (New York: McGraw-Hill, 1960).

36. For a comprehensive discussion of the issue, see my *International Economics of Control* (London: Macmillan; and New York: Halstead-Wiley, forthcoming in 1975).

37. Thomas Gladwin and John Welles, "Environmental Aspects of Multinational Corporate Planning," in my *Studies in International Environmental Economics* (New York: Wiley-Interscience, forthcoming in 1976).

38. See Barnet and Müller, *op. cit.;* and my *Environmental Control and Consumer Protection* (Washington, D.C.: Center for Multinational Studies, Occasional Paper No. 2, 1972).

39. See the discussion contained in S. Chee and K. S. Mun, *op. cit.* See also Richard W. Moxon, *Offshore Production in Less Developed Countries: A Case of Multinationality in the Electronics Industry* (New York: New York University Institute of Finance, 1974). Conventional analyses of costs and benefits of multinationals for developing countries have not considered this issue. See, for example, Louis T. Wells, Jr., "Social Cost/Benefit Analysis for MNCs," *Harvard Business Review* (March–April 1975).

40. See, for example, Jack Baranson, *Industrial Technologies for Developing Countries* (New York: Praeger, 1969); and Organization for Economic Cooperation and Development, *Pilot Survey of Technical Assistance by Private Enterprise* (Paris: OECD, 1967). Also see Raymond Vernon, "International Investment and International Trade in the Product Cycle," *Quarterly Journal of Economics* (May 1966).

41. See Robert G. Hawkins, "Technology Transfer and Multinational Firms: The Home Country Perspective," prepared for OECD symposium on technology diffusion, February 1975 (mimeograph). Also see the following: C. A. Michalet, *Transfer of Technology and the Multinational Firm* (Paris: OECD document DAS/SPR/73.64, 1973); Edwin Mansfield, "Technology and Technological Change," in John Dunning, ed., *Economic Analysis and the Multinational Enterprise* (London: Allen & Unwin,

1974); Keith Pavit, "The Multinational Enterprise and the Transfer of Technology," in John Dunning, ed., *The Multinational Enterprise* (London: Allen & Unwin, 1971).

42. U. N. Balasubramanyam, *International Transfer of Technology to India* (New York: Praeger, 1973).

43. Perhaps the most striking case is U.S. investment in Canada. See Canadian Forum, *A Citizen's Guide to the Gray Report* (Toronto: New Press, 1971); A. E. Safarian, *Foreign Ownership of Canadian Industry* (New York: McGraw-Hill, 1966); and John Fayerweather, *Foreign Investment in Canada: Prospects for National Policy* (New York: International Arts & Sciences Press, 1973).

44. Cf. W. G. Friedmann and G. Kalmanoff, *Joint International Business Ventures* (New York: Columbia University Press, 1961); and Samuel Pisar, *Coexistence and Commerce* (New York: McGraw-Hill, 1970).

45. Cf. Jagdish Bhagwati, *Illegal Transactions in International Trade* (Amsterdam: Elsevier, 1975).

46. See, for example, Ronald Müller, "The Political Economy of Global Corporations and National Stabilization Policy," in George Ball, ed., *Global Companies: The Political Economy of World Business* (Englewood Cliffs, N.J.: Prentice-Hall, 1975).

47. Donald Macaluso, "Multinational Corporations and National Monetary Policy," unpublished Ph.D dissertation, New York University, 1975. Also see John Helliwell, *Public Policies and Private Business* (Oxford: Clarendon Press, 1968).

48. See Alsaaty, *op. cit.,* for a case in point. Also see Arnold W. Sametz, "The Foreign Multinational Company in the U.S.A.," in Jules Backman and Ernest Bloch, eds., *Multinational Companies, Trade and the Dollar* (New York: New York University Press, 1974); as well as C. Fred Bergsten, "Coming Investment Wars?" *Foreign Affairs* (October 1974).

49. One company's efforts are outlined in some detail by Exxon Corporation in *Multinational Enterprise* (New York: Exxon Corporation, 1974).

50. Thomas A Wolf, *U.S. East-West Trade Policy* (Lexington, Mass.: D. C. Heath, 1973).

51. See Richard A. Jackson, ed., *The Multinational Corporation and Social Policy* (New York: Praeger, 1974).

52. Cf. Raymond Vernon, *Sovereignty at Bay, loc. cit.* The United States Overseas Private Investment Corporation (OPIC), for example, which insures foreign investments of U.S. multinationals against expropriation, will refuse to make good on claims resulting from illegal actions in host

countries. On the other hand, the Hickenlooper Amendment is aimed at abolishing foreign aid to any country that fails to make "prompt and reasonable" compensation for nationalized assets of American firms.

53. For some indication of what has been accomplished thus far, see USA-BIAC Committee on International Investment and Multinational Enterprise, *Provision of Data on MNC Operations* (New York: USA-BIAC, 1974).

54. Cf. United Nations Economic and Social Council, *The Impact of Multinational Corporations on the Development Process and on International Relations* (New York: United Nations document E/5500/Add. 1, June 1974), and the background staff report by the Department of Economic and Social Affairs, *Multinational Corporations in World Development* (New York: United Nations document E.73 II.A.11, August 1973). Also see Don Wallace, ed., *International Control of Investment* (New York: Praeger, 1974).

OTHER BOOKS IN THIS SERIES:

BUSINESS PROBLEMS OF THE SEVENTIES
Edited by Jules Backman, Research Professor of Economics, New York University

This volume contains contributions by the following outstanding authorities in the field:
A Foreword by Harold S. Geneen, Chairman and Chief Executive Officer, International Telephone and Telegraph Company
Martin R. Gainsbrugh, Formerly Chief Economist, The Conference Board
Solomon Fabricant, Professor of Economics, New York University
C. Fred Bergsten, Senior Fellow, The Brookings Institution
Simon H. Whitney, Visiting Professor of Economics, Baruch College, City University
M. A. Adelman, Professor of Economics, Massachusetts Institute of Technology
Jesse W. Markham, Harvard University, Charles Edward Wilson, Professor of Business Administration
Lee Loevinger, Partner, Hogan and Hartson, Attornies at Law

ADVERTISING AND SOCIETY
Edited by Yale Brozen, Professor of Business Economics, Graduate School of Business, University of Chicago

This volume contain contributions by the following other scholars in the field:
Daniel J. Boorstin, Smithsonian Institution
Lester G. Telser, University of Chicago
Phillip Nelson, State University of New York at Binghamton
Harold Demsetz, University of California at Los Angeles
Richard A. Posner, University of Chicago
Robert Pitofsky, New York University, Georgetown Law School
John A. P. Treasure, J. Walter Thompson Company
Philip Kotler, Northwestern University

MULTINATIONAL CORPORATIONS, TRADE AND THE DOLLAR
Edited by Jules Backman and Ernest Bloch, New York University

This volume contains contributions from the following other scholars in the field:

Charles P. Kindleberger, Ford Professor of Economics, Massachusetts Institute of Technology

Raymond Vernon, Herbert F. Johnson Professor of International Business Management, Graduate School of Business Administration, Harvard University

Arnold W. Sametz, Professor of Finance, New York University

LABOR, TECHNOLOGY, AND PRODUCTIVITY
Edited by Jules Backman, Research Professor of Economics, New York University

This volume contains contributions by the following other scholars in the field:

Emanuel Stein, Professor of Economics, Humanities, and Social Sciences, New York University

David L. Cole, Chairman, National Commission for Industrial Peace

Peter F. Drucker, Marie Rankin Clarke Professor of Social Science, Claremont Graduate School, Claremont, California

John W. Kendrick, Professor of Economics, The George Washington University

LARGE CORPORATIONS IN A CHANGING SOCIETY
Edited by J. Fred Weston, Professor of Business Economics, Graduate School of Management, University of California, Los Angeles.

This volume also contains contributions by the following leading scholars in the field:

Oscar Grusky, Professor of Sociology, UCLA

Marc Nerlove, Professor of Economics, University of Chicago

Oliver E. Williamson, Professor of Economics, University of Pennsylvania

Richard A. Posner, Professor of Law, University of Chicago

Sidney M. Robbins, Professor of Finance, Columbia University

Robert B. Stobaugh, Professor of Business Administration, Harvard University

Neil H. Jacoby, Professor of Economics and Policy, Graduate School of Management, UCLA

Michael Granfield, Assistant Professor of Business Economics, Graduate School of Management, UCLA

Ronald H. Coase, Professor of Economics, University of Chicago Law School